CONTENTS

DEDICATION 2

FOREWORD 3

SAFETY MESSAGE 4

ABOUT THE AUTHOR 5

LOCATION MAP 6–7

LOCATIONS

LONDON BRIDGE. 8
PORTSEA BACK BEACH. 9
SORRENTO BACK BEACH 10
ST PAULS BACK BEACH 11
DIAMOND BAY BACK BEACH. 12
KOONYA BACK BEACH. 13
ST ANDREWS BEACH 14
RYE OCEAN BEACH 15
GUNNAMATTA SURF BEACH #1 16
GUNNAMATTA SURF BEACH #2 17
WEST HEAD ROCKS 18
FLINDERS PIER. 19
SHOREHAM BEACH. 20
POINT LEO SURF BEACH. 21
MERRICKS BEACH. 22
BALNARRING BEACH 23
SOMERS BEACH 24
STONY POINT PIER. 25
HASTINGS JETTY 26
CANNONS CREEK 27
WARNEET JETTY. 28
BLIND BIGHT JETTY 29
EVANS INLET – TOORADIN 30
SAWTELLS INLET – TOORADIN. 31
CARDINIA CREEK 32
DEEP CREEK 33
BUNYIP RIVER. 34
LANG LANG BEACH. 35
STOCKYARD POINT. 36
GRANTVILLE JETTY. 37

TENBY POINT 38
CORINELLA PIER. 39
SETTLEMENT POINT 40
CORONET BAY. 41
KENNEDY POINT 42
BASS RIVER 43
NEWHAVEN JETTY. 44
RHYLL JETTY 45
SILVERLEAVES 46
COWES PIER 47
RED ROCKS POINT 48
McHAFFIE POINT. 49
FLYNNS REEF. 50
CAT BAY. 51
COWRIE BEACH. 52
KITTY MILLER BAY 53
BERRY'S BEACH 54
CUNNINGHAM BAY 55
ANZAC & CAPE WOOLAMAI BEACHES 56
MAGIC LANDS. 57
RED POINT 58
CLEELAND BIGHT 59
SAN REMO JETTY 60
KILCUNDA SURF BEACH 61
CEMETERY BEACH. 62
POWLETT BEACH 36
WILLIAMSONS BEACH 64
FLAT ROCKS 65
ANDERSONS INLET. 66
VENUS BEACHES 1–5 67

FISHING KNOTS 68

LANDBASED FISHING RIGS 71

BAIT PRESENTATION 74

TARGET FISH ID GUIDE 76

DEDICATION

This book is dedicated to all those landbased anglers looking for somewhere new to explore. Landbased fishing usually begins at a young age and becomes highly addictive and while some may advance and explore from a boat, some continue on the journey to strive to catch that 'fish of a lifetime' from the stones.

To all those that have fished with me over the years and taken the time to share their knowledge I thank you deeply and look forward to the next time we hit the sand together.

To my beautiful wife Angie and children Asha-Marie and Kyla, you have been very understanding and approving of my adventures. I can't thank you enough for your patience and love you with all my heart. And to my Nanny, who happily dropped me off at Sorrento and Portsea ocean beaches or at the Portsea pier from such a young age – you contributed to my fishing addiction… for that I thank you and love you.

First published 2013
Reprinted 2015

Published and distributed by
AFN Fishing & Outdoors
PO Box 544 Croydon, Victoria 3136
Telephone: (03) 9729 8788 Facsimile: (03) 9729 7833
Email: sales@afn.com.au
Website: www.afn.com.au

©Australian Fishing Network 2013

ISBN: 9781 8651 3229 7

Printed in China

first met Jarrod Day almost a decade ago when he presented himself to me in my Tackleworld store in Cranbourne. He was looking for a change in lifestyle and was keen to make fishing his new career.

I noted his enthusiasm and 'can do' attitude very early and knew he was destined to 'make waves' within the fishing industry.

He started photojournalism shortly after and in rapid time he has become one of the country's leading fishing writers. I travel a lot, and it is almost impossible to scan the fishing magazines in any Australian airport newsagency without seeing his big cheesy grin and a thumping fish on one or more of the covers.

This book is a breath of fresh air for landbased anglers in Victoria. They make up such a large percentage of the fishing public, yet are so often over looked by the industries media.

Jarrod's publication works on the KISS principle, (Keep It Simple Stupid) and this is its greatest asset.

Armed with the easy to read layout, simple instructions and specific information, the landbased angler can now hit the beach, rocks and/or pier with confidence of actually catching a fish, rather than just hoping to.

Jarrod has done an incredible job on this quality publication and he should be very proud. I truly hope his efforts inspire you to spend more time on the water with your family and friends having fun, because at the end of the day, that is what life is all about.

Yours in fishing,

Paul Worsteling

Tackleworld Cranbourne
IFISH with TACKLEWORLD

Safety must be forethought

Fishing from the sand, stones or piers is a very enjoyable and relaxing form of fishing, yet some anglers take it to the extreme. Attempting to access dangerous and inaccessible locations just to catch a fish isn't just dangerous but a silly idea. Regardless of where you're fishing, safety must and should be forethought before venturing to a location. If you're fishing from a pier with children, have them wear a life jacket. If you're fishing from the rocks near the ocean, wear a life vest yourself or if you're walking on rocks to the edge of the water, wear the appropriate foot attire or you could get yourself in a very sticky situation.

There are a few locations I specifically haven't written about in this book, purely because they should not be fished. One such location known as 'Punch Bowl' has seen many anglers swept from the rocks and killed; no fish is worth that.

Regardless of where you're fishing, tell your loved ones or a friend where you're going. Take the appropriate safety gear and don't overload yourself with too much gear.

Fishing should be fun and enjoyable and not be the end of a life. The next time you hit the stones, think before you step.

Good luck and fish hard,

Jarrod Day

My say

Fishing along the Mornington Peninsula coastline was a regular occurrence during school holidays while growing up. I spent countless hours dangling a line from the end of the timber, hoping to catch anything; just a fish of some description and I was extremely happy. If it wasn't Portsea or Sorrento pier it was one of the many back beaches that good ol' granny would drop me off to. Either that or I'd take a long hike with a rod in my hand without a care in the world. Exploring the coastline became a real obsession and I quickly gained great respect for the water and its inhabitants. Despite countless empty handed trips, I still found my love for fishing growing by the day. With my passion for fishing growing, I began to explore further, working my way right around the coastline. Many years later I've found myself right in the thick of the industry. While only a hobby back then, it's now my job and a fabulous lifestyle.

I worked in various roles in the I.T industry before becoming a qualified retail manager for Woolworths. Spending almost 10 years in the job, my most prized catch of all became my wife.

While fishing took a back seat for a few years apart from the odd dangle with mates, my wife and I experienced a magnificent day out fishing the Daintree River while on our honeymoon in Port Douglas. Upon returning, I found myself resigning from my role at Woolworths only to take up a job at Tackleworld Cranbourne. The role re-ignited my passion for fishing and this time I grabbed it with both hands. I went back to exploring our local waters at every chance that I could.

Today, I still work at Tackleworld Cranbourne as well as photographing and writing about my adventures, both in Australia and abroad.

I have been fortunate enough to have been a special guest on IFISH with Tackle World (ONE HD), Hooked with Dave Buttfield, Youfish (CH 31), That's Fishing (CH31) and 100% Pure Fishing on Foxtel. I regularly contribute a weekly fishing report on 3AW, Friday's at 7.10 pm and 3 MDR, Wednesday Mornings at 7.30 am.

In the world of photographic journalism I also contribute magazine articles for Victorian Fishing Monthly, South East and West Fishing, Bream Barra and Bass, Country to Coast Journal, Go-Fishing, Saltwater Fishing Australia, Fishing Tips and Techniques, TrailerBoat Fisherman, NAFA, Photofish, Freshwater Fishing and Sportfishing Australia magazines.

While I enjoy being on the water, the real passion is seeing our younger generation enjoy a pastime that is close to my heart. Now with children of my own, there is nothing better than sitting on the edge of a river bank or sandy beach watching them wind in a fish and seeing that priceless smile.

I'll see you on the sand,

Jarrod Day

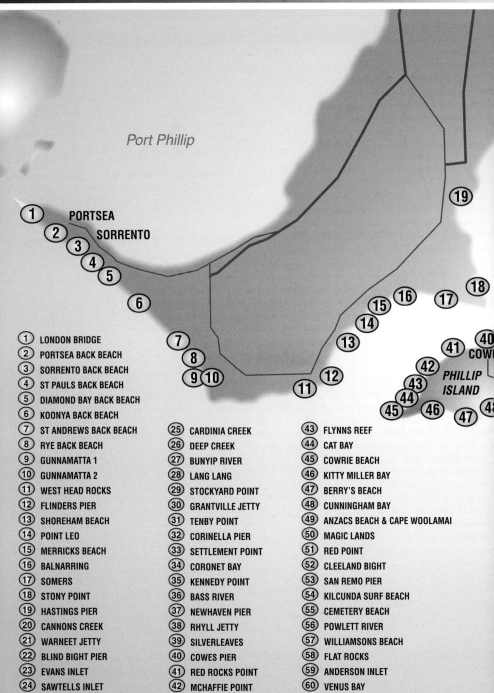

Port Phillip

PORTSEA
SORRENTO

COWE
PHILLIP
ISLAND

1. LONDON BRIDGE
2. PORTSEA BACK BEACH
3. SORRENTO BACK BEACH
4. ST PAULS BACK BEACH
5. DIAMOND BAY BACK BEACH
6. KOONYA BACK BEACH
7. ST ANDREWS BACK BEACH
8. RYE BACK BEACH
9. GUNNAMATTA 1
10. GUNNAMATTA 2
11. WEST HEAD ROCKS
12. FLINDERS PIER
13. SHOREHAM BEACH
14. POINT LEO
15. MERRICKS BEACH
16. BALNARRING
17. SOMERS
18. STONY POINT
19. HASTINGS PIER
20. CANNONS CREEK
21. WARNEET JETTY
22. BLIND BIGHT PIER
23. EVANS INLET
24. SAWTELLS INLET

25. CARDINIA CREEK
26. DEEP CREEK
27. BUNYIP RIVER
28. LANG LANG
29. STOCKYARD POINT
30. GRANTVILLE JETTY
31. TENBY POINT
32. CORINELLA PIER
33. SETTLEMENT POINT
34. CORONET BAY
35. KENNEDY POINT
36. BASS RIVER
37. NEWHAVEN PIER
38. RHYLL JETTY
39. SILVERLEAVES
40. COWES PIER
41. RED ROCKS POINT
42. MCHAFFIE POINT

43. FLYNNS REEF
44. CAT BAY
45. COWRIE BEACH
46. KITTY MILLER BAY
47. BERRY'S BEACH
48. CUNNINGHAM BAY
49. ANZACS BEACH & CAPE WOOLAMAI
50. MAGIC LANDS
51. RED POINT
52. CLEELAND BIGHT
53. SAN REMO PIER
54. KILCUNDA SURF BEACH
55. CEMETERY BEACH
56. POWLETT RIVER
57. WILLIAMSONS BEACH
58. FLAT ROCKS
59. ANDERSON INLET
60. VENUS BAY

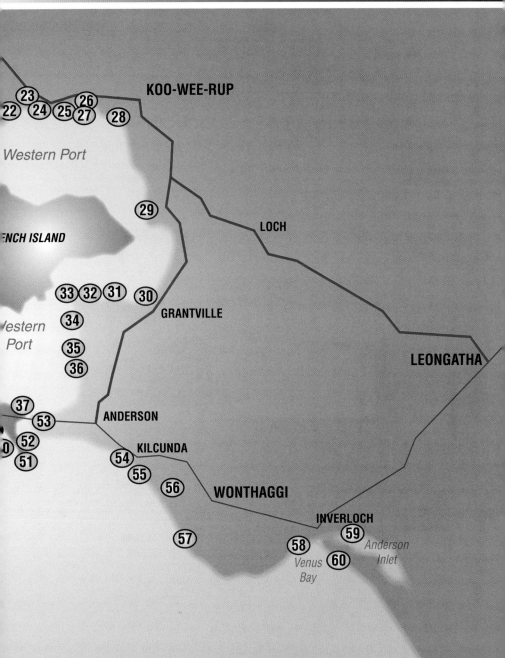

LONDON BRIDGE

🔍 HOW TO GET THERE

London Bridge Road, Portsea. Follow the Point Nepean Road into Portsea. Turn left onto Back Beach Road and follow until you reach the London Beach Road turn off on the right. Follow through until you reach the car park.

🔍 SNAPSHOT

PLATFORM
ROCK

TARGET FISH
SNAPPER
LEATHERJACKET
SWEEP
WRASSE
AUSTRALIAN SALMON

BEST BAIT
PIPI
PILCHARDS
SQUID HEADS
BLUEBAIT
WHITEBAIT
PRAWN
EEL
TREVALLY FILLET
SALMON FILLET

BEST LURES
METAL SLUGS
SOFT PLASTICS
SURF POPPERS

BEST TIMES
LOW TIDE

SEASONS

Snapper
September to February

Leatherjacket
Year round

Sweep
Year round

Wrasse
Year round

Australian salmon
April to August

London Bridge is the last fishable beach with easy access along the Mornington Peninsula coast. This section of the coast is more rock fishing than beach fishing requiring anglers to be very careful as the rocks are extremely slippery during a low tide. This is one location not for the kids. During the low tide, anglers have access to the edge of the rocks where they can fish the drop-off. This drops into five metres of water where the reef meets the sand. London beach should only be fished in light winds from a northerly or easterly direction.

TACTICS
From the car park, the walk to the rocks is around 150 m so don't take too much gear with you. When conditions are right to do so, fish the edge of the rocks casting out towards Bass Strait. To attract sweep in numbers, berley with finely cut pieces of pilchard and sprinkle into the water consistently. The most successful approach to fishing here is using unweighted baits. This can be done by placing three BB split shot sinkers onto your leader followed

by a size 8 long shank hook. The sinkers should be around 30 to 40 cm away from the hook. To be able to fish unweighted baits a light outfit is required. A 7 ft 2 to 4 kg rod with a 3000 size reel and 10 lb braid will suit.

BAITS AND LURES
Pipi, prawn and small pieces of pilchards are ideal for sweep, leatherjacket and wrasse. Use whole bluebait or whitebait when targeting salmon, whole pilchards or squid heads are ideal for snapper. Casting lures is also effective for salmon.

BEST TIDE/TIMES
Two hours either side of the low tide change is a must. Before venturing here look at the weather, swell and wind direction. Northerly winds are favourable with minimal swells a must.

AMENITIES
There are public toilets adjacent to the car park. The nearest shop is located at Portsea back beach or in the main street of Portsea.

KIDS AND FAMILIES
Not suitable for kids.

FINALLY
The fishing here is red hot during certain times of the year. You will need to pick the correct weather conditions to fish comfortably. As this area has slippery rocks, take and wear a life vest and rock boots to avoid falling over or into the water.

PORTSEA BACK BEACH

HOW TO GET THERE

Back Beach Road, Portsea. From the Point Nepean Road, turn left into Back Beach road and follow through until you reach the bottom car park.

SNAPSHOT

PLATFORM
SURF/ROCK

TARGET FISH
AUSTRALIAN SALMON
SWEEP
TREVALLY
YELLOW-EYE MULLET
GUMMY SHARKS

BEST BAIT
PILCHARD
PIPI
MUSSEL
BLUEBAIT
WHITEBAIT
FISH FILLETS
CURED EEL

BEST LURES
METAL LURES
SOFT PLASTIC MINNOWS
SURF POPPERS

BEST TIMES
TWO HOURS EITHER SIDE OF THE TIDE CHANGE, DAWN AND DUSK.

SEASONS

Australian salmon
April to August

Sweep
Year round

Trevally
April to August

Yellow-eye mullet
Year round

Gummy shark
Year round

The Portsea Back beach is a very popular surf beach during the summer months with swimmers and surfers but the fishing during this time is quite poor. When the salmon arrive in the winter months, this beach doesn't get overcrowded like that of other Mornington Peninsula beaches; allowing anglers plenty of gutters to fish. This section of beach is approximately two kilometres in length with three main gutters. Not as deep as some beaches, it is quite shallow but does see good runs of salmon and silver trevally.

TACTICS

Due to the shallowness of this beach, it is best fished in strong southerly winds when the waves carve the gutters deeper. This is when the salmon really fire and with a blend of berley anglers can experience mind-blowing fishing action. A paternoster rig tied from 15 lb trace works well with 1/0 bait holder hooks ideal for salmon. When tying this rig, one bait holder hook should be tied to the top dropper and a long shank size 8 hook on the bottom dropper

to catch silver trevally at the same time. Most fish can be caught on pipi baits whereby bluebait and whitebait are best suited for salmon. Spinning for salmon amongst the surf is also a popular affair and allows anglers to cover more of the area to locate the fish.

BAITS AND LURES

Salmon are best targeted with pilchard, bluebait and whitebait. Trevally and mullet are very responsive to pipi and gummy sharks are attracted to oily fish baits and cured eel.

BEST TIDE/TIMES

Two hours either side of a tide change will usually produce the best results. Fish overcast days or into the night for best results on salmon and gummy sharks.

AMENITIES

There is a public toilet block located in each car park. There is also a surf lifesaving club and café open during summer.

KIDS AND FAMILIES

An ideal location to take the kids fishing although constant supervision is required due to strong swells and currents.

FINALLY

A productive winter fishery for salmon and less crowded than nearby beaches.

SORRENTO BACK BEACH

🔍 HOW TO GET THERE

Ocean Beach Road, Sorrento. From the main street in Sorrento (Ocean Beach Road) follow to the end roundabout and continue straight ahead until you reach the lower car park.

🔍 SNAPSHOT

PLATFORM
SURF/ROCK

TARGET FISH
AUSTRALIAN SALMON
SILVER TREVALLY
YELLOW-EYE MULLET
LEATHERJACKET

BEST BAIT
PIPI
BLUEBAIT
WHITEBAIT
PILCHARDS

BEST LURES
METAL LURES

BEST TIMES
HIGH TIDE FOR THE BEACH AND LOW TIDE FOR THE ROCKS

SEASONS

Australian salmon
April to August

Silver Trevally
April to August

Others
Year round

Sorrento Back Beach is a popular swimming and surfing location throughout the summer months. It is a relatively smaller beach with a rocky sandy bottom. The average depth is approximately 2 to 3 metres. This beach can be difficult to fish but can be productive during the winter months.

TACTICS

Surf outfits are recommended enabling longs casts into the deeper water. Due to the large amount of rocks in the area, snagging up is almost impossible to avoid. With this in mind, anglers should take a back-up of rigs. When targeting these species, a paternoster rig tied from 15 lb trace will suffice. Hook size will differ from species to species with a long sank size 6 for sweep and trevally and a bait holder size 1/0 for the salmon. These species are best targeted when the tide is low. This will allow anglers to walk onto the rocks to further their casts. Ideally, berley is an effective method used to attract fish to the area.

BAITS AND LURES

Most fish can be caught using pipi but salmon are usually caught when using bluebait, whitebait or pilchards. Spinning with metal lures is also productive.

BEST TIDE/TIMES

It is important you fish the high tide when targeting salmon from the beach. Other species can be taken from the rock ledge to the right of the beach but care must be taken.

AMENITIES

There are good amenities at Sorrento back beach including a public toilet block, adequate car parking, picnic tables and a café which operates during the summer months.

KIDS AND FAMILIES

This is a good safe beach to take the kids with plenty of sand to explore. Unexpected waves and strong currents exist thus constant supervision is advised.

FINALLY

A very popular location for surfers and anglers alike. Fish the tides stated above for best results.

ST PAULS BACK BEACH

HOW TO GET THERE

St Pauls Road, Sorrento. From Point Nepean Road, turn left into St Pauls Road and follow to the car park.

SNAPSHOT

PLATFORM
ROCK

TARGET FISH
SWEEP
AUSTRALIAN SALMON
WRASSE
SILVER TREVALLY
SNAPPER
BARRACOUTA

BEST BAIT
BLUEBAIT
WHITEBAIT
PIPI
PILCHARDS

BEST LURES
METAL LURES
SURF POPPERS
SOFT PLASTICS

BEST TIMES
LOW TIDE

St Pauls back beach is a true rock fishing location so anglers must be very careful when fishing here. Rock boots or shoes with cleats should be worn for safety reasons. This location should not be fished in southerly winds. From the sand it is very shallow averaging 30 cm to 1 m on the high tide. In order to fish this location successfully, anglers will need to fish this beach on a low tide and make their way out onto the rocks to the edge where it drops away to four metres.

TACTICS

The main species from this location are silver trevally and sweep which can be quite sizeable. The most effective way to fish here is when the wind and swells are low. An onion bag containing pellets can be hung over the edge and anglers can cast unweighted strips of squid or pilchard fillets into the berley trail. This is an extremely effective technique that will lead to good catches of fish. The most effective rig is a size 6 long shank hook tied to a length of 10 lb trace with three BB size split shot sinkers crimped to the line for a little added weight. As you don't have to cast long distances to catch fish, a light 7 ft 2 to 4 kg rod will suit.

BAITS AND LURES

Pipi, bluebait, whitebait, pilchards and pipis are all effective baits to use in this location. Smaller offerings are better so don't go too big.

BEST TIDE/TIMES

This location is best fished two hours either side of the low tide as anglers require access to the rock ledge.

AMENITIES

There are no amenities in the area. The nearest shops are located a few hundred metres away on St Pauls Road.

KIDS AND FAMILIES

This isn't a location to take the kids fishing.

FINALLY

A top location in calm conditions for the experienced rock angler.

SEASONS

Sweep
All year round

Australian salmon
April to August

Wrasse
Year round

Silver Trevally
April to August

DIAMOND BAY BACK BEACH

🔍 HOW TO GET THERE

Diamond Bay Road, Sorrento. From Melbourne Road, turn down Diamond Bay Road and follow to the car park.

🔍 SNAPSHOT

PLATFORM
SURF/ROCK

TARGET FISH
AUSTRALIAN SALMON
SILVER TREVALLY

BEST BAIT
PIPI
BLUEBAIT
WHITEBAIT
PILCHARDS
SQUID

BEST LURES
SOFT PLASTIC
MINNOWS &
CREATURES

BEST TIMES
LOW TIDE

SEASONS

Salmon
April to August

Silver trevally
April to August

Diamond Bay is a very small fishing location almost locked off by ocean swells. On a high tide, this area is very shallow reaching a maximum of only 1 m in depth while during a low tide; you can wade out onto the rocks and cast into 5 m just beyond the reef. The rocks are terribly slippery so care must be taken at all times. The prime times to fish here is the last hour of the run out tide and first hour of the run in tide.

TACTICS

Diamond Bay isn't known as being a good fishing location but does offer some excellent silver trevally fishing from time to time. Berley is essential to bring the fish into the bay. The best spot to fish is right at the bottom of the stairs as there is a sandy channel that runs between the two reefs. Although surf outfits can be used, light spin tackle is also an option. Anglers can cast and retrieve soft plastics here with great success too. Metal lazer lures are also worth casting to get out to the deeper reefs where salmon can be lurking. Light surf rods and braided lines are perfect for this location. The best type of hook for trevally is a size 6 long shank.

BAITS AND LURES

Pipis, bluebait, whitebait and pilchard fillets are all very good and will secure a good catch. Soft plastic minnows and metal lures are worth using if you're into lure fishing.

BEST TIDE/TIMES

Low tide is productive if you wade out towards the reef. High tide is also good but you will have limited locations to fish as the waves come right up the beach to the bottom of the stairs.

AMENITIES

There are no amenities in the area. A take away food shop is located near the corner of St Pauls Road and Melbourne Road.

KIDS AND FAMILIES

This beach is not recommended to take kids fishing. Although the surroundings are picturesque there isn't much for them to do and it can become dangerous on the rocks.

FINALLY

This is a good beach to fish from if you pick the right tides and time of year. Perfect for a relaxing fish and if you get amongst the trevally you'll have a ball.

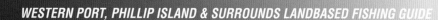

KOONYA BACK BEACH

HOW TO GET THERE

Hughes Road, Blairgowrie. From either Point Nepean Road or Melbourne Road, turn onto Hughes Road and follow to the top car park. The beach is a short walk from here.

SNAPSHOT

PLATFORM
SURF/ROCK

TARGET FISH
AUSTRALIAN SALMON
WRASSE
OCEAN SWEEP
SILVER TREVALLY

BEST BAIT
PIPI
CALAMARI STRIPS
PILCHARDS
BLUEBAIT
WHITEBAIT

BEST LURES
METAL SLUGS
SOFT PLASTIC MINNOWS
SURF POPPERS

BEST TIMES
HIGH AND LOW TIDES, DAWN AND DUSK

SEASONS

Australian salmon
April to August

Silver trevally
April to August

Others
April to August

Koonya Back Beach has two parts to it separated by a small rocky outcrop. Both sections of this beach fish very well during the year. The beach features sections of reef but is mostly sand with an average depth of around three metres. The section of beach to the left has a very large sandy channel running from the shoreline right out into Bass Strait. This is a great location to target salmon and silver trevally.

TACTICS

While Koonya is quite a shallow surf beach it does get good runs of respectable fish. Silver trevally are a common catch here and tend to be in abundance throughout autumn until the end of winter. While the majority of these fish range 30 to 40 cm, 50 cm models can be caught. Pipi's tend to be the most favoured bait when fished on a paternoster rig tied from 10 to 15 lb trace. Silver trevally have small mouths so a long shank size 6 hook will suit. During the winter, salmon are also in abundance with a high tide preferred. They can be caught using the same paternoster rig as for the trevally but upgrade the hook to at least a 1/0 bait holder. Surf poppers can be used and generally work quite well.

BAITS AND LURES

Salmon respond well to bluebait, pipi, whitebait and pilchards as well as soft plastics and metal slugs. Wrasse aren't fussy while silver trevally and sweep can be caught on pipi and small pieces of pilchard fillets.

BEST TIDE/TIMES

Fish two hours either side of the high tide. Dawn or dusk is good for all species especially when the salmon are around.

AMENITIES

A public toilet block is located in the lower car park.

KIDS AND FAMILIES

A good place to take serious fisho's but there are better places to take kids that are new to the sport.

FINALLY

Fishing from the rock platform can be very productive and a host of species can be encountered amongst the reef.

ST ANDREWS BEACH

🔍 HOW TO GET THERE

Ocean Drive, Rye.
From Point Nepean Road, turn right into Dundas Street and follow for approximately six kilometres. Turn right into Bass Meadows Boulevard and follow to the end car park.

🔍 SNAPSHOT

PLATFORM
SURF/ROCK

TARGET FISH
GUMMY SHARKS
AUSTRALIAN SALMON
SILVER TREVALLY
YELLOW-EYE MULLET

BEST BAIT
BLUEBAIT
WHITEBAIT
PIPI
PILCHARD FILLET

BEST LURES
SURF POPPERS
METAL LURES
SOFT PLASTICS

BEST TIMES
LOW TIDE FOR SALMON, HIGH TIDE FOR GUMMY SHARKS.

SEASONS

Australian salmon
April to August

Silver trevally
April to August

Yellow-eye mullet
Year round

Gummy sharks
Year round

St Andrews Beach is a relatively shallow stretch of beach with three main gutters. After a heavy southerly blow, these gutters can become quite deep and average five metres. The rest of the beach averages 1 to 2 metres. There are patches of heavy reef in which anglers must be wary of when attempting to land fish. A high tide is the most productive time to catch fish during the lead up to the full and new moons.

TACTICS

With the extensive offshore reefs close to St Andrews, it can boast some of the best night time gummy fishing along this stretch of coast. A running or fixed sinker rig is ideal and should be tied from 80 lb trace. Due to the pressure of the surf break, anglers should also stick to using circle hooks to aid in keeping the fish connected to the rig.

When targeting salmon, a paternoster rig tied from 20 lb leader with size 1/0 long shank hooks is ideal.

BAITS AND LURES

The most effective baits for gummies are fresh salmon fillet, trevally fillet, tuna fillet and cured eel. Salmon and silver trevally will take bluebait, whitebait and pipi. They can also be chased on metal lures and surf poppers.

BEST TIDE/TIMES

St Andrews beach fishes best for gummy sharks in the evenings during a rising tide from January through to March. Low tide is a very productive time to fish for salmon as it allows anglers to see the edge of the reef to cast over.

AMENITIES

There are no amenities in the area; however, take away food shops can be found on Point Nepean Road in Rye.

KIDS AND FAMILIES

Not the best location for children due to slippery rocks and unexpected swells.

FINALLY

St Andrews provides a good platform for chasing salmon during the day and gummy sharks after the sun drops.

RYE OCEAN BEACH

HOW TO GET THERE

Paradise Drive, Rye. From Nepean Highway, turn left into Truemans Road and right into Sandy Rd. Follow Sandy Rd turning left into Bass Meadows Boulevard. This will take you onto Paradise Drive which will turn into a car park at its end.

SNAPSHOT

PLATFORM
SURF

TARGET FISH
AUSTRALIAN
SALMON
YELLOW-EYE
MULLET
SNAPPER

BEST BAIT
WHITEBAIT
PIPI
PILCHARD
CALAMARI
SALMON
TREVALLY
EEL FILLETS

BEST LURES
BLUE AND RED
SURF POPPERS
METAL SLUGS
SOFT PLASTICS

BEST TIMES
HIGH TIDE, DAWN
OR DUSK

SEASONS

Australian salmon
April to August

Yellow-eye mullet
Year round

Gummy sharks
Year round

Snapper
Spring

Tucked away behind the Rye Golf Club, Rye ocean beach is a little gem when it comes to fishing for salmon and gummy sharks. This beach has a few very deep gutters with nearby reefs which attract fish during the autumn and winter months. The beach is around 2 m deep with some of the gutters up to 4 m deep within a reasonable cast of the shore. Rye ocean beach fishes best on a high tide when the fish can push in close.

TACTICS

When targeting salmon, a paternoster rig tied from 20 lb trace best suits due to the nearby reef which anglers can get hung up on losing their catch and rig. Hook size can vary but a size 1/0 bait holder will suit. Bluebait, whitebait or pipi will get the job done. Gummy sharks are highly prized in the surf and this stretch of coast can yield some quality fish. The prime time to target gummies is of an evening during a rising tide. If berley is used, they will find your selected gutter and offered baits. Either a running sinker rig or fixed sinker rig is suitable and should be tied from 80 lb trace. A solid hook is required in either a 6/0 suicide or circle pattern.

BAITS AND LURES

Cured eel, silver trevally fillet, tuna fillet and salmon fillet are gun baits for gummy sharks. Salmon respond well to pipi, bluebait, whitebait and surf poppers, metal lures and soft plastics.

BEST TIDE/TIMES

For most species, a high tide is most productive, especially during dawn or dusk. Arrive at low tide to see where the rocks and reef are located.

AMENITIES

There are public toilets located in the car park and shops are located a 5 to 10 minute drive up the road.

KIDS AND FAMILIES

Ocean swells and strong currents exist so adult supervision is required at all times.

FINALLY

A productive beach, especially during winter. When fishing this location, a northerly wind direction will suit. Southerlies and westerlies make fishing difficult as the swells and side wash make fishing very difficult.

GUNNAMATTA SURF BEACH #1

🔍 HOW TO GET THERE

Truemans Road, Rye. From Point Nepean Road in Rye turn left into Truemans Road. Follow until you see the first car park turn off on the right.

🔍 SNAPSHOT

PLATFORM
SURF/ROCK

TARGET FISH
AUSTRALIAN SALMON
YELLOW-EYE MULLET
SILVER TREVALLY

BEST BAIT
PIPI
BLUEBAIT
WHITEBAIT
PILCHARD FILLET
PRAWNS

BEST LURES
METAL SLUGS
SURF POPPERS

BEST TIMES
TWO HOURS EITHER
SIDE OF A HIGH
TIDE.

SEASONS

Australian salmon
April to August

Yellow-eye mullet
Year round

Silver trevally
April to August

Beach number 1 fishes fairly similar to beach 2 except for a rocky outcrop to the left of beach number one. This section of the beach is very deep due to the waves washing in and dragging the sand between the rocks back out which creates more cover for the fish to hide in.

TACTICS

Fishing this location will require surf rods of 11 ft or longer with 4500 to 8000 size reels. Main lines should be a minimum of 25 lb line if fishing monofilament and 10 lb if fishing with braid. Leaders should be tied from at least 40 or 60 lb for abrasion resistance against the rocks. The standard setup is a paternoster rig tied from 30 or 40 lb trace. Tying two droppers will enable two fish to be caught at a time. Salmon can be caught on 1/0 bait holder hooks while mullet and trevally can be caught when using size 6 to 10 long shank hooks.

BAITS AND LURES

Salmon are best targeted with bluebait, whitebait and pipi. Prawns can also be used and do work well but do have a tendency to fall off during a cast. Pilchard fillets are worthwhile too as all species will take them. Pipi and mussel baits are very good when fishing for mullet and silver trevally.

BEST TIDE/TIMES

The most productive time to fish around the rocks is usually two hours either side of the high tide change. Fishing the low tide can be productive but smaller fish will often be encountered.

AMENITIES

There is a public toilet block located in the car park.

KIDS AND FAMILIES

Gunnamatta surf beach 1 is a great location to take the kids fishing. Strong currents and unexpected waves do exist so adult supervision is paramount. The rocks can also be very slippery at all times, care must be taken.

FINALLY

If you're after a good catch of fish then this location will deliver during the right time of year.

Truemans Road, Rye. From Point Nepean Road at Rye turn left into Truemans Road and follow until you reach the end car park.

SNAPSHOT

PLATFORM
SURF

TARGET FISH
GUMMY SHARK,
AUSTRALIAN
SALMON
YELLOW-EYE
MULLET

BEST BAIT
PIPI
PILCHARDS
BLUEBAIT
WHITEBAIT
EEL FILLET
SALMON
TREVALLY FILLET
TUNA FILLET
SQUID HEADS
CALAMARI STRIPS

BEST LURES
METAL LURES
SURF POPPERS
SOFT PLASTICS

BEST TIMES
HIGH TIDE AT NIGHT

SEASONS

Gummy sharks
Year round

Australian salmon
Winter

Yellow-eye mullet
Year round

Silver trevally
Winter

Stretching for approximately 18 km, Gunnamatta surf beach is a sandy beach with myriad gutters spread along its entire length. To the left, many of the gutters contain reef which attracts a wide range of species. Deep gutters form here on a regular basis and the best way to identify them is by standing at the top of the sand dunes while looking for dark blue water between the white wash.

TACTICS

If you intend on targeting gummy sharks, a rod rated to 15 kg with a reel that is capable of holding 300 m of 25 lb line is ideal. Most of the time there are large shore breaking waves which will require anglers to use 80 lb trace when rigging a running or fixed sinker rig. Hook sizes ranging from 6/0 to 8/0 in a suicide or circle hook design are recommended. Salmon, mullet and silver trevally can be caught when using either 1/0 bait holder hooks or size 10 long shank hooks tied onto a paternoster rig along with. Lure anglers can also catch quality salmon from any of the gutters. A 7 to 9 ft lure casting rod

with a 4000 series reel loaded with 10 lb braid is recommend for this. Metal lures work very well when retrieved at high speed.

BAITS AND LURES

Gummy sharks like big oily baits such as eel fillet, salmon, trevally and tuna fillet, squid strips or squid heads. If you catch a salmon, fillet it and cast it out as a fresh fillet bait for best results. For salmon, mullet and trevally use either pipi, pilchards, bluebait or whitebait. Surf poppers, metal lures and soft plastics can also be used for salmon.

BEST TIDE/TIMES

A high tide early in the morning is very productive when targeting salmon and trevally, overcast days are equally as productive. Gummy shark fishing should only be conducted at night during a rising tide. Fishing around a full moon will increase your chances.

AMENITIES

There is a public toilet block located in the large car park near the surf life saving club.

KIDS AND FAMILIES

Gunnamatta surf beach is a great location to take the kids fishing. There are no take away food shops close by, so being prepared will be very important. Strong currents and unexpected waves do exist so adult supervision is paramount.

FINALLY

A great location for the family to spend the day or for serious anglers to fish overnight.

WEST HEAD ROCKS

🔍 HOW TO GET THERE

Golf Links Road, Flinders. From Frankston-Flinders Road continue on to Wood St. At the roundabout turn left into Cook St and follow around turning right into Golf Links Road. Turn left into the car park overlooking the ocean. There are stairs to the right that access the beach.

🔍 SNAPSHOT

PLATFORM
ROCK

TARGET FISH
KING GEORGE
WHITING
SILVER TREVALLY
SALMON
WRASSE
LEATHERJACKET

BEST BAIT
BLUEBAIT
WHITEBAIT
SQUID
PIPI

BEST LURES
METAL LURES
SOFT PLASTIC
MINNOWS

BEST TIMES
HIGH TIDE DURING A
NORTHERLY WIND.

SEASONS

King George whiting
Warmer months

Silver trevally
Winter

Salmon
Winter

Others
Year round

Also known as Flinders Back Beach, West Head Rocks is a very productive fishery. This location must be fished on a high tide; otherwise anglers will experience a lot of snags on the rocks with very little fish caught. The bottom is solid reef and averages three metres in depth. The most productive fishing will be during a northerly wind as the swell will be flat. The rocks are also very slippery and care must be taken.

TACTICS

Due to the rocky terrain, a 10 to 12 ft surf rod is recommended. These rods will generally feature the strength required to bring in fish and control them around the rocks. Reel should be in a 6000 to 8000 series and be spooled with at least 30 lb braid with 50 lb recommended. Keeping in mind the snaggy territory, anglers should use a paternoster rig with a spoon sinker attached. The reason for the spoon is to eliminate snagging in the rocks. The paternoster rig should be tied from 20 lb trace. Hooks for these species will vary with a long shank size 6 suitable for leatherjacket, whiting and silver trevally while a bait holder or suicide hook in a 3/0 size will suit wrasse and salmon.

BAITS AND LURES

Good all-purpose baits include squid, pipi and pilchard. Wrasse and leatherjacket aren't fussy and will steal baits quickly so be prepared to strike straight away.

BEST TIDE/TIMES

High tide is preferred as too is a northerly wind which will keep swells down.

AMENITIES

There are no amenities in the immediate area.

KIDS AND FAMILIES

Due to the terrain and ocean swells this is not a location recommended for children.

FINALLY

The fishing from West Head Rocks can be challenging and tends to get anglers frustrated due to the large amount of snags. If you persist however; the fishing can be sensational.

FLINDERS PIER

HOW TO GET THERE 🔍

The Esplanade, Flinders. Follow Bass Street, the pier is at the end.

SNAPSHOT 🔍

PLATFORM
PIER

TARGET FISH
WHITING
SQUID
LEATHERJACKET
SALMON
PIKE
BARRACOUTA
PARROTFISH

BEST BAIT
SILVER WHITING
SALMON
MULLET
PIPI
MUSSEL
BASS YABBIES

BEST LURES
METAL LURES
SOFT PLASTIC
WORMS
SQUID JIGS

BEST TIMES
EARLY MORNING
AND LATE EVENING
ON A HIGH TIDE.

SEASONS

Squid
September to December

King George whiting
December to February

Others
Year round

Flinders pier is quite a popular fishing location for anglers wishing to catch calamari. This location fishes well all year and can be exceptional from September to November when the large spawners arrive. Some calamari can be up to three kilograms in weight which can test light tackle. It is a high tide that fishes best as the calamari move in closer to the pier; the depth is around 5 to 6 metres. There is plenty of weed patches in which the calamari hide and spawn. The nearby sand patches are also known for holding good numbers of whiting throughout the year. Ideally, you should fish calmer weather when here. Easterlies and southerlies hamper the fishing while northerlies and westerlies don't affect it.

TACTICS

Though the majority of this area ranges from 5 to 10 m deep, the bottom is relatively sandy with thick seagrass interspersed. A baited jig with silver whiting used for bait works very well and should be suspended 1 to 2 m off the bottom. Anglers fishing with artificial jigs can walk the length of the pier casting and retrieving. This technique works very well both at night and during the day. A paternoster rig is most effective when fishing for whiting. Either tie it from 10 or 15 lb trace with 1/0 circle hooks or size 6 long shanks for best results. Grass whiting, silver trevally and leatherjackets will also be caught on the same rig and will also take the same baits offered. They are greedy scavengers that are generally caught as a by-catch.

BAITS AND LURES

Some of the squid taken here can reach over three kilograms so full fish baits suspended on a prong under a float are ideal. Artificial jigs are also productive but don't let them sink too long – the weed is unforgiving here. Squid and pipi work well for King George whiting.

BEST TIDE/TIMES

The prime time to be fishing this location is on a high tide early in the morning. High tide at dawn or dusk can produce excellent numbers of whiting.

AMENITIES

Public toilets, rubbish bins, car parks and shops are located in the main street of Flinders.

KIDS AND FAMILIES

A great location to take the kids but supervision is required as the pier sits quite high above the water. A playground is located nearby.

FINALLY

This pier is very popular for big squid and for good reason too. While popular in the warmer months it also fishes well in winter.

SHOREHAM BEACH

🔍 HOW TO GET THERE

Beach Road, Shoreham. Follow Frankston-Flinders Road and turn left into Beach Road, follow to the car park.

🔍 SNAPSHOT

PLATFORM
BEACH

TARGET FISH
GUMMY SHARKS
PIKE
SNOOK
YELLOW-EYE MULLET
SEVEN GILL SHARKS

BEST BAIT
CALAMARI
TUNA FILLET
SALMON FILLET
TREVALLY FILLET
EEL FILLET
PIPI
PILCHARD

BEST LURES
DEEP DIVING LURES
METAL LAZER LURES

BEST TIMES
HIGH TIDE, NIGHT TIME.

SEASONS

Gummy sharks
Year round

Pike and snook
Year round

Yellow-eye mullet
Year round

Shoreham Beach is relatively shallow and is mostly sandy with very few weed patches. The depth ranges from 1 to 3 m within an easy cast from the beach. Due to the shallowness of this beach, it fishes best on a high tide. There is plenty of area anglers can fish and it can accommodate many without becoming over crowded.

TACTICS

Shoreham Beach is known for its amazing gummy shark fishing from time to time. This usually occurs on the lead up to a full moon from January to March. With very little structure to be busted off on, anglers can use lighter leader. A running sinker rig tied from 40 lb trace is recommended with 6/0 suicide hooks ideal. Cured eel, tuna, salmon and trevally fillets are all effective baits. There are also plenty of whiting that can be targeted at this location and can be easily caught. Paternoster rigs suit here as anglers will be able to cast them quite a distance. They should be tied from 15 lb leader with either size 6 long shank hooks or 1/0 circle hooks. Pipi and squid strips are the most effective baits and a three ounce sinker is ideal.

BAITS AND LURES

Gummy sharks will take oily fish baits as well as squid and eel. Mullet can be caught when using pipi or pilchard fillets and metal lures or soft plastics are ideal for the pike and snook.

BEST TIDE/TIMES

Two hours either side of the high tide is productive but when fishing for gummy sharks, fish during a run in tide at night. Fish around the full moon for best results on gummies.

AMENITIES

There is a public toilet block situated adjacent to the car park. BBQ facilities and a picnic area are also available on the foreshore reserve.

KIDS AND FAMILIES

This location is fantastic for the kids. It is a safe beach and there are plenty of amenities nearby.

FINALLY

An easy location to fish with the potential of producing some big gummies.

POINT LEO SURF BEACH

HOW TO GET THERE 🔍

Western Parade, Point Leo. Take Point Leo Road (becomes Western Parade) to the life saving club.

SNAPSHOT 🔍

PLATFORM
BEACH

TARGET FISH
TARGET SPECIES
SALMON
GUMMY SHARKS
FLATHEAD

BEST BAIT
PILCHARD
PRAWN
SQUID
SALMON FILLET
EEL FILLET
WHITEBAIT
BLUEBAIT

BEST LURES
METAL LURES
SOFT PLASTIC
SHADS

BEST TIMES
LOW TIDE AT NIGHT,
AND THE TOP OF
THE HIGH TIDE.

SEASONS

Flathead
Year round

Australian salmon
Year round

Gummy sharks
Winter

Point Leo surf beach is a great fishery for a wide range of species. This location should be treated as a surf beach but also has a very large rock feature to its left which attracts plenty of fish. From the surf, anglers can cast into 3 m of water while from the rocks it is 5 metres deep. It is very weedy around the rocks; causing plenty of snags while the beach itself is sand.

TACTICS

From either the beach or the rocks, gummy sharks are targeted but tend to favour pushing in close during the night. A high tide is recommended when the wind isn't blowing too hard to hamper the fishing. Ideally, a northerly wind is preferred here. Running sinker rigs are highly recommended as they enable the bait to sit near the bottom. This can be tied from 80 lb trace with a single 6/0 circle hook

working well. Flathead and salmon can be caught with a paternoster rig tied from 20 lb line. Surf rods in the 10 to 12 ft range are recommended here.

BAITS AND LURES

The most effective baits for gummy sharks are tuna fillet, salmon fillet, trevally fillet, cured eel and calamari strips. For flathead try prawns and whole pilchards or bluebait. Salmon respond to pipi, bluebait and whitebait as well as surf poppers.

BEST TIDE/TIMES

For gummy sharks, the bottom of the low tide at night is best whereas a run in tide is best for salmon and flathead. Try fishing on an overcast day for salmon, they will be more prolific.

AMENITIES

There is a public toilet block located near the life saving club. You can camp on the foreshore reserve where there is also a BBQ facility.

KIDS AND FAMILIES

Children must be supervised here. It is a relatively safe location but care must be taken as strong currents exist.

FINALLY

Persistence is the key; this spot produces some big flathead and gummy sharks.

MERRICKS BEACH

🔍 HOW TO GET THERE

Merricks Beach Road, Merricks. Follow Frankston-Flinders Road to Merricks Beach Road. Park at the end car park.

🔍 SNAPSHOT

PLATFORM
BEACH

TARGET FISH
GUMMY SHARKS
WHITING
SALMON

BEST BAIT
PILCHARD
EEL
PIPI
BLUEBAIT
TUNA
CUTTLEFISH
BASS YABBIES
SQUID
WHITEBAIT

BEST LURES
BEST LURES
METAL LURES
SOFT PLASTICS
BLADES

BEST TIMES
HIGH TIDE.

SEASONS

Gummy sharks
Winter

King George whiting
November to April

Australian salmon
Winter

This location is extremely weedy but yields some great catches of gummy sharks in season. The depth is around 3 to 4 m with a few sand patches where whiting can also be targeted. Either side of the beach are rocky points, though these hold fish they can be very snaggy and difficult to fish at times.

TACTICS

Successful gummy shark fishing from this location tends to be undertaken during the night. Due to the shallowness of this area, gummies often frequent the weedy beach after dark. Anglers wanting to fish for gummies can do so with a 12 ft heavy surf rod to enable a long cast. Main lines should be at least 30 lb (braid) as there are some large sting rays in the area. This rig should be tied from at least 60 lb

trace with 80 lb recommended. A single 6/0 circle hook works well. Gummy sharks can be fussy with baits so have a variety on hand. This includes squid, cured eel, salmon, trevally and tuna fillet. Whiting are frequently caught during the summer months with the prime times at least two hours either side of a high tide change. A paternoster rig works well with size 6 long shank hooks.

BAITS AND LURES
Gummy sharks can be fussy with baits so have a variety on hand. This includes squid, cured eel, salmon, trevally and tuna fillet. King George whiting respond well to pipi and fresh squid.

BEST TIDE/TIMES
A high tide early in the morning will produce good results as will a rising tide at night. Brave the weather in winter for some big fish.

AMENITIES
Public toilets are located near the yacht club.

KIDS AND FAMILIES
The beach is sandy and flat, and children are able to swim there as strong currents are rare in the immediate area.

FINALLY
During the holiday season this area remains relatively quiet at night making it a great proposition for anglers chasing gummy sharks.

BALNARRING BEACH

HOW TO GET THERE

Foreshore Road, Balnarring. The quickest way to Balnarring Beach is to turn left off Sandy Point Road onto Balnarring Beach Road. Once you reach the Balnarring general store, turn left into Foreshore Road and follow to the Yacht club car park.

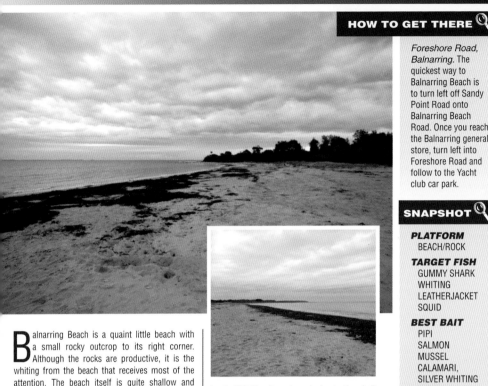

SNAPSHOT

PLATFORM
BEACH/ROCK

TARGET FISH
GUMMY SHARK
WHITING
LEATHERJACKET
SQUID

BEST BAIT
PIPI
SALMON
MUSSEL
CALAMARI,
SILVER WHITING
TUNA
SILVER TREVALLY

BEST LURES
SQUID JIGS

BEST TIMES
HIGH AND LOW TIDE.

Balnarring Beach is a quaint little beach with a small rocky outcrop to its right corner. Although the rocks are productive, it is the whiting from the beach that receives most of the attention. The beach itself is quite shallow and sandy with patches of weed beds scattered within casting distance. From the beach you'll be casting into approximately two metres of water but in season, King George whiting and leatherjackets make up the bulk of the catch. Fishing from the rocks can yield a good catch of calamari in calm weather along with gummy sharks when fishing the high tide. This area can be very snaggy which will require anglers to take a good selection of sinkers.

TACTICS

Despite there being some weedy patches spread about, you can pretty much fish right along the length of the beach. A paternoster rig with long shank size 6 or Black Magic KL 1/0 hooks will suit best. When beach fishing for whiting a longer rod is preferred and something in the 10 ft range with a light tip is ideal. There is little current at this location so a four ounce sinker will be ideal. Furthermore, you will require a set of waders if you're wishing to gain a further cast. The rocks to the right of the beach are quite popular with anglers searching out gummy sharks and do fish particularly well during the winter months. It is recommended that the rocks be fished on low tide. Gummy sharks are a bottom feeder so a running sinker rig will suit best. This should be tied from 60 lb trace with a 6/0 size circle

hook. If fishing for calamari, due to the shallow water it is wise to use a baited squid prong rather than an artificial jig.

BAITS AND LURES

Gummy sharks prefer oilier baits whereby tuna, calamari, salmon and trevally strips are ideal. Whiting will take both mussel and pipi baits along with strips of squid. If squid are targeted with bait, use silver whiting.

BEST TIDE/TIMES

A high tide in the evening is very productive for whiting. If you're fishing during winter for gummy shark, fish the last two hours of the run out tide and first two hours of the run in tide. Squid are best targeted on the high tide at night.

AMENITIES

Located in the car park is a toilet block and a milk bar is situated on the main road.

KIDS AND FAMILIES

This beach is fantastic for the whole family; however, it is not recommended that children be taken onto the rocks.

FINALLY

A great location to take the family and get amongst some great fish.

SEASONS

King George whiting
Summer

Leatherjackets
Summer

Gummy sharks
Year round

Squid
Year round

SOMERS BEACH

🔍 HOW TO GET THERE

Parklands Avenue, Somers. Park on Parklands Avenue, from here you will need to walk down The Promenade to the beach.

🔍 SNAPSHOT

PLATFORM
BEACH

TARGET FISH
FLATHEAD
SNAPPER
SHARKS
WHITING
MULLET
TREVALLY
LEATHERJACKET
PARROTFISH
GARFISH
SALMON
PIKE
RED MULLET
SQUID

BEST BAIT
FRESH FISH FILLETS
PILCHARD
PRAWN
PIPI
MUSSEL
SQUID
EEL

BEST LURES
SOFT PLASTICS

BEST TIMES
RUN-OUT TIDE,
NIGHT TIME.

SEASONS

Sharks
September to March

Snapper
September to December

Pinkie snapper
November to April

Trevally
Winter

King George whiting
Summer months

Others
Year round

Somers is an excellent landbased fishery, particularly for gummy sharks. This area can be fished from a few locations which all hold the same species. Along the rock wall at the Somers Yacht Club anglers can cast into two metres of water where the bottom is a mixture of sand and weed. There are a few sandy channels that fish often swim up in search of food. Furthermore, anglers can walk to the left of the beach to fish off the rocks. Out from here, the depth is around two metres as well with a deeper drop-off within a cast. This has a rocky ledge in which plenty of fish can be caught just beyond.

TACTICS

When fishing for gummies a running sinker rig works well although a fixed sinker rig is often better allowing casting of the rig easier to control. This rig should be tied from 80 lb trace with a 5/0 suicide hook or 6/0 circle ideal. Using a circle hook will help to eliminate bit offs from toothy sharks such as seven gillers. Switching to wire leaders can often turn gummies off from your baits so it isn't recommended. If elephants are the chosen target, then tie the rig from 30 lb trace with a 3/0 suicide or circle hook. Whiting can also be caught for those specifically targeting them and this can be done with the use of a paternoster rig ties from 15 lb trace. Due to the length of the casts required to access deeper water, a 12 ft surf rod is recommended.

BAITS AND LURES

Most of the fish respond well to a variety of baits with squid, cured eel fillet, trevally, salmon and tuna fillet all working well. Elephants like smaller, softer baits where strips of squid, half pilchards or pipi's are recommended.

BEST TIDE/TIMES

At night, the last three hours of the run in tide fishes better, as gummy sharks feed higher on the flats in search of a meal. The run out tide fishes better for whiting.

AMENITIES

There are no amenities in the immediate area.

KIDS AND FAMILIES

A safe beach for the family to spend the day; however, the water can become quite weedy at times.

FINALLY

One of the best beaches to fish from on a warm balmy night.

STONY POINT PIER

HOW TO GET THERE

Stony Point Road, Stony Point. Follow Stony Point Road to the end car park.

SNAPSHOT

PLATFORM
PIER

TARGET FISH
SQUID
SILVER TREVALLY
GARFISH
YELLOW-EYE MULLET
FLATHEAD
SALMON
WHITING

BEST BAIT
PILCHARD FILLETS
PIPI
MUSSEL
SILVERFISH
DOUGH
PEELED PRAWN
BASS YABBIES
SILVER WHITING

BEST LURES
METAL LURES
SOFT PLASTICS

BEST TIMES
HIGH TIDE AT DAWN AND DUSK.

Stony Point pier is a very solid structure providing anglers with good access into deep water. The pier itself can support many anglers and can become quite busy during the summer months. From the base of the pier, a sturdy hand rail runs its length along the right hand side. There are no hand rails at the end of the pier, making it unsafe for small children. Fishing from the pier can be very productive with snapper and gummy sharks as the main target while whiting, salmon and calamari can be caught from the inside of the pier.

TACTICS

Snapper tend to frequent this area from September through to January. The top of the high tide fishes better than the low as the fish will move onto the nearby reef in search of food. Casting towards the red pylons is your best bet to catch one as there is a small reef that exists next to it. Gummy sharks are a common catch from the pier and require some forethought before catching. If you can fish from the pier without many people around, fish the end corner during the run out tide as this will enable you to access the deeper water. A running sinker rig will allow the bait to sit on the bottom, within reach of a gummy. Hook sizes may vary but either a 5/0 suicide or 6/0 circle is recommended. To catch garfish, a float setup is most effective. A small quill float works best with two BB sized split shot crimped to the line underneath the float. Calamari can be caught year round and are active feeders at night.

BAITS AND LURES

Silver whiting is best for squid, while silver trevally, yellow-eye mullet, flathead and salmon prefer pilchard, pipi and mussel. Live Bass yabbies and tenderised calamari strips are good for King George whiting. Gummy sharks and snapper will respond to oily fish baits.

BEST TIDE/TIMES

Approximately 1.5 hours either side of the high tide is ideal for all species. Fish into the night for your best chance at cracking a gummy or snapper.

AMENITIES

A general store is located opposite the pier. A caravan park, public toilets, fish cleaning facilities, rubbish bins, V-Line train station, and car park are all nearby. A small fee sometimes applies to park your car during the summer months.

KIDS AND FAMILIES

This is a great spot for kids and families alike especially with the Stony Point Caravan Park nearby.

FINALLY

The pier provides access to a good variety of fish and is a suitable location for the family to enjoy the day.

SEASONS

Squid
September to December

Silver trevally
October to March

Yellow-eye mullet
Year round

Flathead
Year round

Australian salmon
Year round

King George whiting
October to March

HASTINGS JETTY

🔍 HOW TO GET THERE

Skinner Street, Hastings. Follow Marine Parade until it turns into Skinner Street. Continue along Skinner Street. The jetty is located at the first car park.

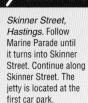

🔍 SNAPSHOT

PLATFORM
PIER

TARGET FISH
KING GEORGE WHITING
MULLET
TREVALLY
SALMON
FLATHEAD
MULLOWAY

BEST BAIT
PIPI
BASS YABBIES
PILCHARD FILLET
PRAWN

BEST LURES
METAL LURES
SOFT PLASTIC
MINNOWS

BEST TIMES
HIGH TIDE AT DUSK.

SEASONS

Silver trevally
Winter

Bay trout
Spring

King George whiting
Summer

Others
Year round

The Hastings jetty is situated right in the heart of the Hastings channel which averages four metres in depth. On one side, anglers have access into the channel while on the inside of the jetty; anglers can cast towards the marina. The bottom is mostly mud but still attracts plenty of fish worth targeting.

* At the time of writing this, the Hastings pier was under repair. They had removed the end of the pier to fit new pylons and walking platform. Once built, this will offer anglers a more comfortable platform to fish from.

TACTICS

There are many different techniques that will work from the pier but the simplest methods are often them most successful. All species can be caught when using a paternoster rig tied from 15lb leader. Hooks size should be kept small with a long shank size 6 ideal for all species except mulloway whereby a larger hook will be required. Berley is essential to attract fish to your area. Mulloway are the most highly sort and although elusive, are a popular catch from the pier. Anglers that seek mulloway tend to fish for them on the lead up and lead down to a full moon. Live baits should be rigged on a running sinker rig. This should be tied from 80 lb trace with a suicide size 6/0 hook ideal.

BAITS AND LURES

Live baiting for mulloway is the preferred method with salmon and calamari top baits. If live baits are unobtainable then fresh calamari rings are a great alternative. Pipis, Bass yabbies and pilchard fillet are effective for trevally, salmon and whiting.

Salmon can also be caught on metal lures and/or soft plastics in minnow patterns.

BEST TIDE/TIMES

Tide changes are most successful at this location. Early morning produces better catches of trevally and mullet. Try an afternoon run-in tide when targeting whiting or after dark for mulloway.

AMENITIES

There is a toilet block located 400 m to the right of the jetty car park. An indoor swimming pool, with a café inside is located at the start of the jetty. Rubbish bins are also provided.

KIDS AND FAMILIES

A great location to teach children how to fish but as always supervision is required.

FINALLY

An extremely productive platform during a high tide for a wide variety of species.

CANNONS CREEK

HOW TO GET THERE

*Irene Parade,
Cannons Creek.*
From Baxter-Tooradin
Road, turn into
Cannons Creek Road
and follow it all the
way to the end, then
turn right onto the
gravel road.

SNAPSHOT

PLATFORM
PIER

TARGET FISH
MULLOWAY
YELLOW-EYE
MULLET
SILVER TREVALLY
KING GEORGE
WHITING

BEST BAIT
LIVE MULLET
AND SALMON
PILCHARD FILLET
PIPI
MUSSEL
BASS YABBIES

BEST LURES
LARGE SOFT PLASTIC
PROFILES

BEST TIMES
HIGH TIDE AT NIGHT.

Cannons Creek is the back end of the Warneet estuary system. It is quite tidal and during a low tide is almost a trickle of water. With this in mind, a high tide is the prime time to fish as they make their way back onto the shallows in search of food. The area is lined with mangroves and has a soft muddy bottom.

TACTICS

Though the fish here are not large in any scale, it is a good location to catch fresh bait for other adventures. Salmon, silver trevally, flathead, yellow eye mullet and the odd whiting are caught. The most widely used rig is a paternoster rig but a running sinker rig is suggested due to the depth of the area. This should be tied from light leader such as 8 or 10 lb with a size 10 long shank hook working well. When fishing this location, all the mentioned species can be caught in the same area. Pipi and pilchard fillets work very well when cast into the main body of the channel. In this case, you will have to sit back and wait for a fish as using berley is practically impossible. A nibble tip rod is ideal in this location.

BAITS AND LURES

Casting large soft plastics for mulloway can be rewarding, as can live baiting with mullet and salmon. Pilchard fillets, pipis, mussels and Bass yabbies will attract mullet, trevally and whiting.

BEST TIDE/TIMES

As mentioned high tide is the only time to fish this location.

AMENITIES

Other than a car park near the jetty, no immediate amenities are available.

KIDS AND FAMILIES

Not an ideal location for kids as there isn't a lot for them to do.

FINALLY

An almost hidden location that can produce some good fish at high tide.

SEASONS

Yellow-eye mullet
Year round

Salmon
SpringYear round

Silver trevally
November to April

King George whiting
Spring and summer

Flathead
Year round

WARNEET JETTY

🔍 HOW TO GET THERE

Rutherford Parade, Warneet. From Baxter-Tooradin Road, turn onto Warneet Road and follow signs to the boat launching facility. Look for the long jetty next to the boat ramp.

🔍 SNAPSHOT

PLATFORM
PIER

TARGET FISH
YELLOW-EYE MULLET
SILVER TREVALLY
FLATHEAD
KING GEORGE
WHITING

BEST BAIT
PIPI
MUSSEL
BASS YABBIES
SOFT PLASTICS

BEST LURES
SOFT PLASTIC
WORMS AND GRUBS
SQUID JIGS

BEST TIMES
HIGH TIDE AT DUSK
AND DAWN ARE
PEAK.

SEASONS

Yellow-eye mullet
Year round

Silver trevally
November to April

Flathead
October to April

King George whiting
November to March

The sleepy town of Warneet can deliver some amazing fishing from the local pier from time to time. The pier stretches from the boat ramp and extends into the middle of the Rutherford Inlet channel. This provides anglers with access to deep water which at its end averages three meters deep on the top of the high tide. The current can run quite hard, requiring anglers to fish with heavy sinkers. The most effective time to fish is two hours either side of the high tide.

TACTICS

In recent years, the pier has been an exceptional location in which to catch calamari. They tend to be in good numbers surrounding the lead up to a full and new moon. While a baited jig will work, artificial jigs are by far the most effective. Smaller jigs in the 2.5 size range in varying colours work well. Throughout the year, whiting, flathead, salmon and silver trevally are all common catches when anglers are using berley to bring them to the area. These fish can be caught using a paternoster rig tied from 10 lb trace. Hook sizes will vary between species but a good all-rounder is a long shank size six.

BAITS AND LURES

Pilchard fillets cut into small pieces will attract mullet, trevally and flathead. Pipi, mussel and Bass yabbies are best for whiting. Squid is a good all-round bait but will need to be cut into small pieces when used. Casting and retrieving soft plastics with a quick 'lift and pause' technique, or just a slow wind is effective on flathead here too.

BEST TIDE/TIMES

Fishing 1.5 hours either side of the high tide is essential. If this coincides with dusk or dawn, trevally are an excellent possibility. Mullet and flathead can be taken throughout the day.

AMENITIES

Public toilets and a BBQ area are located approximately 250 m from the pier. A tap is situated at the end of the pier and a rubbish bin can be found in the car park vicinity – use this for discarding your bait packaging!

KIDS AND FAMILIES

In general, this is a good location; however the pier is very narrow so care needs to be taken. Mosquitoes and sand flies are abundant, so repellent is necessary.

FINALLY

Well worth a visit, with good fishing to be had. Fishing the high tide is a must due to the limited water level during low tide.

BLIND BIGHT JETTY

HOW TO GET THERE

Anchorage Drive, Blind Bight. From Baxter-Tooradin Road, turn onto Warneet Road, then left onto Blind Bight Road. The pier is adjacent to the picnic area and toilets.

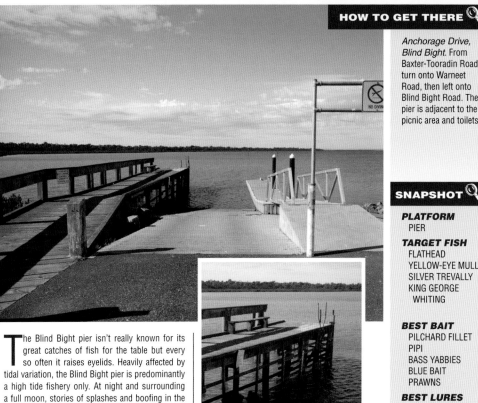

SNAPSHOT

PLATFORM
PIER

TARGET FISH
FLATHEAD
YELLOW-EYE MULLET
SILVER TREVALLY
KING GEORGE
WHITING

BEST BAIT
PILCHARD FILLET
PIPI
BASS YABBIES
BLUE BAIT
PRAWNS

BEST LURES
SOFT PLASTICS IN
PADDLE TAIL AND
GRUB PATTERNS.

BEST TIMES
HIGH TIDE AT DAWN
OR DUSK.

The Blind Bight pier isn't really known for its great catches of fish for the table but every so often it raises eyelids. Heavily affected by tidal variation, the Blind Bight pier is predominantly a high tide fishery only. At night and surrounding a full moon, stories of splashes and boofing in the shallows is a common topic amongst local anglers. This is most likely an elusive mulloway but an extremely rare capture from the pier itself, although it isn't impossible with the right techniques implemented. The bottom surrounding the pier is mostly mud with the surrounding edges thick in mangroves.

TACTICS

In order to attract fish to this location it pays to sprinkle berley on the surface. With the slow force of the current, the light weighted berley will carry over a fair distance attracting fish to the area. A paternoster rig works well and should be tied from 10 lb trace with size 10 long shank hooks. Mullet will take any small pieces of bait used but pilchards are hardly passed up. These can be cut into very small fillets and placed onto the hook. A light sinker in the 1 to 2 oz range will be required. If you choose to use pipis for bait, you will encounter the odd whiting. Unfortunately it is unlikely that you will catch a bag of fish but a good half dozen is an excellent catch from here. Many will be undersize but you will catch a few keepers. For an attempt at a mulloway use fresh bait at night, preferably in summer.

BAITS AND LURES

Soft plastics are effective on flathead and a lift and pause retrieve works well. Pilchard fillet and pipis are both great baits for yellow-eye mullet and silver trevally, as are live Bass yabbies.

BEST TIDE/TIMES

Fishing the high tide is essential due to the lack of water at low tide. Aim to fish days when the high tide coincides with sunrise or sunset.

AMENITIES

A picnic/play area and BBQ are in close proximity, as are toilets and a fish cleaning table. A general store is also nearby.

KIDS AND FAMILIES

A good spot to take the kids fishing thanks to ample room for them to play as well as amenities nearby.

FINALLY

A quiet and comfortable location to drown a bait or two.

SEASONS

Flathead
October to March

Yellow-eye mullet
Year round

Silver trevally
October to March

EVANS INLET – TOORADIN

🔍 HOW TO GET THERE

South Gippsland Highway, Tooradin. Travelling along the South Gippsland Highway you'll come into the township of Tooradin. Within metres of driving over the Inlet bridge there is a service road to your right. Take that and you will see the fishing platform.

🔍 SNAPSHOT

PLATFORM
JETTY

TARGET FISH
YELLOW-EYE MULLET
AUSTRALIAN SALMON
TAILOR
SILVER TREVALLY

BEST BAIT
PIPI
PRAWN
MUSSEL
BLUEBAIT
PILCHARDS

BEST LURES
SMALL SOFT
PLASTICS

BEST TIMES
HIGH TIDE.

SEASONS

Yellow-eye mullet
Year round

Australian salmon
Year round

Tailor
Year round

Silver trevally
Year round

Evans Inlet, on the Southern side of South Gippsland Highway, features a small jetty that anglers can fish from. Although high from the water's surface, it is quite productive for salmon, silver trevally and yellow-eye mullet. This area is best fished on a high tide as during the low it is almost bone dry. Evans Inlet is the beginning of the Tooradin Channel which opens out into Western Port. From the platform you only need to cast five metres to access the middle of the main channel.

TACTICS

A light estuary rod/reel outfit is all that is required when fishing here. If you can use light tackle then do so as the kids will enjoy it a whole lot more. A suggestion is to use six pound line as a maximum. If you're going to search for the perch a graphite 7 ft 2 to 4 kg soft plastics rod with 2500 series reel and 10 lb braid will do the job. A quill float works well with a few split shot sinkers crimped below it for weight. The best sized hook is a long shank size 10 or twelve.

BAITS AND LURES

All of the fish on offer will take any bait offered but pipi, prawn and pilchard fillet works very well. Soft plastics can also be effective when the salmon and trevally are on the chew.

BEST TIDE/TIMES

High tide is the most productive time to fish as there isn't a lot of water to cover the ground on a low tide.

AMENITIES

There is play equipment at the nearby reserve for the kids to play in when the fish are slow. There are shops within a hundred or so metres of walking distance too.

KIDS AND FAMILIES

A good location to take the kids as it is a year-round fishery and there are plenty of smaller fish for them to catch.

FINALLY

A great spot to teach kids how to fish or to collect some bait for a future trip.

SAWTELLS INLET – TOORADIN

HOW TO GET THERE

South Gippsland Highway, Tooradin. Follow the South Gippsland Highway to Tooradin. The inlet is located on the right.

SNAPSHOT

PLATFORM
ESTUARY

TARGET FISH
YELLOW-EYE MULLET
SILVER TREVALLY
KING GEORGE
 WHITING
TAILOR
FLATHEAD
BREAM

BEST BAIT
PIPI
PRAWNS
PILCHARD
MAGGOTS

BEST LURES
SOFT PLASTICS
 WRIGGLERS
SMALL SHALLOW
 DIVING
 HARDBODIES

BEST TIMES
HIGH TIDE AT DAWN
 OR DUSK.

SEASONS

Yellow-eye mullet
Year round

Silver trevally
November to April

King George whiting
November to March

Flathead
October to April

Bream
Year round

Sawtell inlet on the northern side of the South Gippsland Highway is more of an estuary that drains and fills with the tide. This is achieved by a series of pipes which run under the highway. There are myriad of fish in Sawtell but most are very small. Yellow-eye mullet, silver trevally and salmon are in abundance. The entire area is mangrove lined; providing plenty of habitat for fish. For those willing to explore the area, estuary perch is a possible catch.

TACTICS

If you're keen on searching for a perch then you will have to walk the inlet working the snags. This is more effective when casting small hard body lures and soft plastics. Squidgy 80 mm wrigglers in the bloodworm colour are extremely effective along with Yo-Zuri Eba shad hardbody lures. This fishery is a year round affair with the perch becoming more active in the warmer months. For all other species a 2 to 4 kg soft plastic setup will suffice. Fish small baits under a quill float with a size 10 or 12 long shank hook. Berley will aid in attracting the fish to your baits so bring some along and throw in handfuls at a time.

BAITS AND LURES

Most baits will work well here, provided they are small. Pipi, prawn and pilchard fillets will all do well. Soft plastic wrigglers and finesse hardbodies are a great alternative to baits and encourage anglers to explore the entire inlet.

BEST TIDE/TIMES

High tide is advisable during dawn and dusk. During a low tide the inlet is drained of a lot of water which sees fish moving out with it.

AMENITIES

Public toilets, car parking, BBQs, cafés, and a playground are all within walking distance.

KIDS AND FAMILIES

A great location to take the children thanks to the abundance of smaller fish and playground facilities nearby.

FINALLY

A top location to take the family for the day. Many first captures have been taken from here.

CARDINIA CREEK

🔍 HOW TO GET THERE

South Gippsland Highway, Koo Wee Rup. Follow South Gippsland Highway towards Phillip Island. Approximately one kilometre past the Tooradin township is Cardinia Creek. The Western Port side of the road bridge is the most productive area to fish.

🔍 SNAPSHOT

PLATFORM
CREEK

TARGET FISH
YELLOW-EYE MULLET

BEST BAIT
BLUEBAIT
PIPI
DOUGH
PILCHARD

BEST LURES
LURES AREN'T AS EFFECTIVE AS BAIT HERE.

BEST TIMES
HIGH TIDE.

SEASONS

Yellow-eye mullet
Year round

Cardinia Creek is a extremely narrow waterway situated at Koo Wee Rup. The bottom is muddy, with grassy banks on either side. Known to support a huge population of mullet, this location can be very rewarding and provides a great bait gathering location.

TACTICS

A float setup will do the trick here, as will a paternoster rig but fish light. Use a main line of approximately 2 to 3 kg and a light estuary rod. Use a size 10 or 12 long-shank hook for best results.

BAITS AND LURES

Small pieces of bluebait or pilchard work well, as do pipi and tiny balls of dough. Use plenty of berley to attract the fish to your immediate area and once they arrive sporadically throw more in to keep them around.

BEST TIDE/TIMES

A high tide is best as this is when the fish push into the upper reaches in search of food. Dawn and dusk are the best times to plan your trips around.

AMENITIES

There are no amenities in this area.

KIDS AND FAMILIES

Not a great location for kids to fish unless they are really keen. The banks are muddy and lined with grass. The highway is nearby too.

FINALLY

While not the prettiest location, the creek holds a large population of fish.

DEEP CREEK

HOW TO GET THERE

South Gippsland Highway, Koo Wee Rup. Follow the South Gippsland Highway towards Phillip Island. Deep Creek is located approximately 1.5 km past Tooradin, near Cardinia Creek.

SNAPSHOT

PLATFORM
CREEK

TARGET FISH
TARGET SPECIES
YELLOW-EYE MULLET
JUVENILE SALMON
SHORT-FIN EELS

BEST BAIT
PILCHARD FILLET
PIPI
CHICKEN FILLET

BEST LURES
SMALL MINNOW
STYLE SOFT
PLASTICS.

BEST TIMES
HIGH TIDE.

TACTICS
A light estuary rod such as a nibble tips is ideal for the mullet here. Use a float set up with size 10 or 12 long shank hooks laced with small baits for best results. Paternoster rigs are ideal for Australian salmon and the short-fin eels.

BAITS AND LURES
Pilchard fillets, pipis and chicken fillet are all excellent baits. Prawn is also quite good when peeled and used as small segments rather than whole.

BEST TIDE/TIMES
High tide only as it is virtually dry at low tide.

AMENITIES
There are no amenities at this location.

KIDS AND FAMILIES
Not a good location for kids. While an easy place to fish, the banks are muddy and uncomfortable for kids.

FINALLY
A good place to collect bait although it isn't somewhere you would necessarily spend all day at.

SEASONS
Yellow-eye mullet
Year round

Juvenile salmon
November to April

Short-fin eels
**Year round
(especially after heavy rain)**

Deep Creek is a small creek that runs into the upper reaches of Western Port. It is often overlooked as a fishing attraction due to the water colour and very shallow level at low tide. At its deepest, it is only two metres and gets shallower the higher up you go containing a muddy bottom. It is an easily accessible creek directly off the highway.

BUNYIP RIVER

HOW TO GET THERE

South Gippsland Highway, Koo Wee Rup. Between Cardinia Creek and Deep Creek is the Bunyip River. This is the largest river along the South Gippsland Highway.

SNAPSHOT

PLATFORM
RIVER

TARGET FISH
MULLET
TREVALLY
ESTUARY PERCH
SHORT-FIN EELS

BEST BAIT
PILCHARD FILLET
CHICKEN PIECES
FRESHWATER YABBIES
BASS YABBIES
PIPI

BEST LURES
SOFT PLASTIC
WRIGGLERS
SHALLOW DIVING
HARDBODIES

BEST TIMES
INCOMING TIDE AT
DAWN AND DUSK.

SEASONS

Yellow-eye mullet
Year round

Trevally
Winter months

Estuary perch
Summer

Short-fin eels
Spring

The Bunyip River is not very appealing to the eye at first glance but can deliver some very good fishing. Throughout the year, this river system is quite murky in colour due to the muddy bottom which is constantly stirred from the tidal fluctuation. Though it may be dirty, yellow-eye mullet and the odd silver trevally can be caught. There is good bank access either side of the highway bridge and at its deepest point on a high tide it is approximately three metres.

TACTICS

This location has very little sportfish to target, rather it holds a very good population of yellow-eye mullet. Short-fin eels are a common catch in the upper reaches along with the odd estuary perch. It is most productive on the high tide when the fish push further up the system. The most effective technique to catch them is to use a float type rig. This can be tied from 10 lb trace with a quill float working well. The ideal hook for mullet is a long shank size 8 or

ten. A running sinker rig can be used and if so, use a size 1 ball sinker as you won't require heavy sinkers.

BAITS AND LURES

Small baits of pilchard fillet and chicken are ideal for trevally and mullet while eels will take any smelly bait offered. Bloodworm wrigglers are great for estuary perch if you can find them, as is live freshwater yabbies.

BEST TIDE/TIMES

All species should be targeted on the run-in tide. The more water that pushes into this river, the more fish push into the upper reaches. Dawn and dusk will see higher concentrations of fish encountered.

AMENITIES

On the opposite side of the river is a rest stop where small food stalls are set up on weekends. There is a lookout tower and a public toilet block.

KIDS AND FAMILIES

Only suitable for keen young anglers.

FINALLY

The Bunyip River system has plenty of fish on offer throughout the year. While the fish aren't big they can be caught consistently with the use of a good fine berley.

LANG LANG BEACH

HOW TO GET THERE

Jetty Lane, Lang Lang. Follow the Bass Highway towards Phillip Island and turn right on Jetty Lane. There's plenty of car parking available.

SNAPSHOT

PLATFORM
BEACH

TARGET FISH
GUMMY SHARKS
ELEPHANT FISH
FLATHEAD
WHITING
SALMON

BEST BAIT
SQUID
PILCHARDS
CURED EEL
BLUEBAIT
PIPIS

BEST LURES
SOFT PLASTIC SHAD
VARIETIES AND
BLADES.

BEST TIMES
FLOOD TIDE AND
INTO THE NIGHT.

Lang Lang beach is a large shallow mud flat which heads towards French Island. The area is almost dry on a spring low tide, but a decent high tide brings some exceptional fish within casting distance. The surrounding bottom structure is mainly mud and sand and baits will be sitting in only 1 or 2 m of water.

TACTICS

The beach is quite shallow during the high tide but a long cast will put you in the strikezone. When fishing for gummy sharks from this location, a running sinker rig or fixed sinker rig works well and ensures the baits are near the sea floor. These rigs should be tied from 60 or 80 lb trace with size 6/0 suicide or circle hooks. A similar rig can be used when targeting elephant sharks except it is best tied from 40 lb trace with 3/0 size hooks.

BAITS AND LURES

Gummy sharks will take a variety of baits but for best results use cured eel, squid strips and fresh fish fillets. Elephants can be caught using pipi's, pilchards and squid. When targeting mullet, a paternoster rig tied from 10 lb trace with two long shank size 10 hooks. Flathead are suckers for soft plastic lures and blades. Try a large plastic shad in gold or pink. If targeting them with bait, use bluebait, pilchards or squid.

BEST TIDE/TIMES

The top of the tide is a must due to the shallow nature of the beach. A half tide through to a full and an hour or two after is ideal.

AMENITIES

There is a toilet block, undercover BBQ area and Caravan Park nearby.

KIDS AND FAMILIES

The beach is quite a safe location for the kids; there is also plenty of space for them to play.

FINALLY

Whilst not much to look a;t the beach is a very productive fishing location. It can be busy during the Easter holidays when the elephant fish are about in numbers and does allow for easy access to some true Western Port gummies.

SEASONS

Gummy sharks
Year round

Elephant fish
March to May

Flathead
Year round

Salmon and whiting
Summer

STOCKYARD POINT

HOW TO GET THERE

Bay Road, Jam Jerrup. Follow the Bass Highway and turn right into Bay Road. Turn left at the "T" intersection at Foreshore Road. Park at the end of Foreshore Road. Follow the beach to the left to the sand spit – or in peak times, other anglers already fishing there.

SNAPSHOT

PLATFORM
BEACH

TARGET FISH
GUMMY SHARK
SNAPPER
ELEPHANT SHARK
SALMON
TREVALLY
SHARKS

BEST BAIT
CURED EEL
SQUID
TUNA FILLETS
PILCHARD
PIPI
PRAWNS

BEST LURES
METAL LURES
SOFT PLASTIC CURL
TAIL GRUBS

BEST TIMES
LOW TIDE ONLY.

SEASONS

Gummy shark,
Australian salmon
& trevally
Year round

Snapper, school shark &
King George whiting
Summer

Elephant shark
March to May

Tailor
February to May

Stockyard Point is without doubt the most popular landbased location found in Western Port that is consistent year-round. This is a low tide only fishing location that will allow anglers to access the deeper water. Once at the sand spit, anglers can cast into the channel which is around 3 to 4 m in depth. The bottom is mud but yields some great catches of fish. One thing to note is that anglers must walk as far to the right of the spit as possible before walking to its northern most point. If this is not achieved, anglers will find themselves knee or waist deep in thick black mud very quickly.

TACTICS

Gummies tend to be caught mainly during the night on the low tide when they are cruising the edges of the channels for food. The most effective rig is a running sinker tied from 60 lb trace with a single 6/0 circle hook attached. During elephant season from February through to May, elephants can be targeted and caught both during the night and day. They are best to target using a running sinker rig made from 20 lb trace and 3/0 hooks. There are two main outfits that should be used at Stockyard Point. The first, a heavy outfit for the sharks should consist of a 12 ft surf rod with large suitable reel capable of holding 300 m of 50 lb braid. For the second outfit, a 10 ft rod with lighter action will be ideal for all the other species.

BAITS AND LURES

Gummy sharks will take a variety of baits with tuna fillet, salmon, trevally and cured eel all working well. Elephant fish are best to target with squid and pilchards although they aren't very fussy. Food grade prawns are also popular baits here amongst the locals.

BEST TIDE/TIMES

This is a definite low tide only proposition. Around 1.5 hours each side of low tide are the best times. This way you can walk out comfortably onto the sand spit that forms Stockyard Point. From here you can cast into the channel that runs parallel to the beach.

AMENITIES

There are none so bring food and water.

KIDS AND FAMILIES

Not appropriate for children as the sand is soft and muddy. It is also a long distance from the car park.

FINALLY

A great location for landbased sharks. The long walk in is well worth the effort if you crack a big fish. Carrying it back to the car is another issue altogether though.

GRANTVILLE JETTY

HOW TO GET THERE

Pier Road, Grantville. From the Bass Highway turn right at the intersection at Grantville into Pier Road. Follow to the end of the road and you will see the jetty on the left.

SNAPSHOT

PLATFORM
JETTY

TARGET FISH
GUMMY SHARK
ELEPHANT FISH
YELLOW-EYE MULLET
BAY TROUT
SILVER TREVALLY

BEST BAIT
PIPI
PILCHARDS
SQUID HEADS
EEL FILLET
TUNA FILLET
SALMON FILLET

BEST LURES
SMALL METAL LURES

BEST TIMES
HIGH TIDE.

The Grantville jetty is very small when it comes to fishing jetties around Western Port. This location is a high tide fishery only as during the low tide it is bone dry.

This area fishes best from February until the end of May when the elephants are in abundance. Being a small jetty, it can accommodate only one or two anglers at any one time when fishing from its end.

TACTICS

While a mixture of species can be caught including salmon, silver trevally and mullet, the most highly prized species from this location are the elephant fish. A running sinker rig will suit and should be tied from 20 lb trace with a size 3/0 circle or 4/0 suicide hook working well. Anglers should try to cast as far as they can in an attempt to reach some deeper water. While the majority is only 2 to 3 m on a high tide, it is still a productive location.

BAITS AND LURES

Elephants respond to a variety of baits with the most effective being squid, pipi and pilchard. Gummy sharks respond well to squid heads, cured eel fillet, tuna fillet and salmon fillet if fresh.

BEST TIDE/TIMES

This jetty can only be fished at high tide. Fishing at night is the perfect time if you want to target gummies and/or elephant fish.

AMENITIES

There are public toilets located near the jetty. There is also take away food shops located along the Bass Highway.

KIDS AND FAMILIES

Although not highly recommended as a location to take kids, it is safe. In saying that, the pier sits high above the water so constant supervision is required.

FINALLY

A good location to spend the evening if you intend on targeting elephant fish or gummy sharks. Plenty are caught here throughout the year and it is a more productive location than some might think.

SEASONS

Gummy shark
Year round

Elephant fish
February to May

Yellow-eye mullet
Year round

Bay trout
Year round

TENBY POINT

HOW TO GET THERE

Marine Road, Tenby Point. Follow the Bass Highway and turn right on Corinella Road. Turn right into Argent Road, right at Guy Road, then left on Bayview Road. Tenby Point is on the right. Once on the beach, walk right, just past the old pier. Beware of soft mud!

SNAPSHOT

PLATFORM
BEACH/ROCK

TARGET FISH
GUMMY SHARK
SNAPPER
MULLOWAY
ELEPHANT FISH

BEST BAIT
SQUID
CURED EEL
PIPI
PILCHARD
FRESH FISH FILLETS

BEST LURES
DUE TO THE SHALLOW NATURE OF THE BEACH SQUID LURES AREN'T VERY EFFECTIVE.

BEST TIMES
HIGH TIDE AND AFTER DARK. PARTICULARLY AROUND A NEW OR FULL MOON.

SEASONS

Gummy shark
Year round

Elephant fish
March to May

Mulloway
February to May

Tenby Point is situated on the corner of a small Bay just north east of Corinella. It has a mostly mud bottom with a rock groin that juts out into Western Port. The fishing takes place from a small rocky outcrop found at the end of a stretch of rubbly beach. The Tenby Point channel floods the area during the incoming tide. During this time fish move out from the deep channel up onto the shallow mudflats to feed.

TACTICS

The mudflats here are littered with small jagged rocks and as such it is advisable to fish a heavier leader than normal – 60 to 80 lb is ideal. Plenty of good fish have been lost here due to the harsh terrain and it can be heartbreaking. Expect to lose a few rigs and bring plenty of pre-tied ones in your tackle kit. Running sinker rigs with 5/0 to 7/0 hooks work well. A paternoster rig is also useful when targeting elephants and snapper. Use a 3/0 or 4/0 hook for best success – circles are recommended.

BAITS AND LURES

Squid heads and rings, fish fillets and cured eel are all effective for gummy sharks, snapper and elephant fish. Flat fish such as stingrays and banjo sharks are also partial to these offerings and can be a nuisance here. Most of these shallow mudflats also fill with small mullet and salmon which make excellent fresh bait. Use a small piece of pipi or pilchard fillet on a size 10 hook to catch them.

BEST TIDE/TIMES

A couple of hours either side of high tide is the best bet at Tenby Point.

AMENITIES

There are none. Follow Guy Road to Corinella if you are in need of any supplies.

KIDS AND FAMILIES

Not appropriate for children as the rocks are easy to trip on and the walk takes approximately 10 minutes over soft sand. For a close alternative try Corinella Pier instead.

FINALLY

Tenby Point is a great place to target quality gummy sharks and many big fish have been taken here. Mulloway are always a possibility here as they come in the shallows to feed on the flounder.

CORINELLA PIER

HOW TO GET THERE

*Peter Street,
Corinella.* Follow the
Bass Highway and turn
right at Corinella Road.
Turn left onto Smythe
Street and follow to
the Corinella Foreshore
Caravan Park (this
becomes Peter Street).
You can park at the
base of the pier.

SNAPSHOT

PLATFORM
PIER

TARGET FISH
GUMMY SHARK
ELEPHANT FISH
WHITING
MULLOWAY

BEST BAIT
CURED EEL
SQUID
PILCHARD
SAURIES
PIPI

BEST LURES
CREATURE STYLE
SOFT PLASTICS

BEST TIMES
HIGH TIDE AT NIGHT.

C orinella pier is an extremely popular fishing destination throughout the year. The fishing here can be extremely productive on a high tide when fish will travel through the channel within easy casting distance of the pier. The bottom is predominately mud and the current can be quite strong.

TACTICS

Gummy sharks can be caught throughout the year and are willing takers of calamari, pilchards, trevally fillet, salmon fillet and tuna. Gummy sharks are predominantly a bottom feeder thus a running sinker rig will suit. This also applies when fishing for mulloway and elephant fish in season. When tying this rig, use 80 lb trace as you could be run around the pier's pylons. Hooks for gummies can differ but something in the 6/0 to 7/0 range will suffice. When fishing for elephants use a 3/0 circle hook as they only have a small mouth. Anglers wanting to catch the elusive mulloway tend to do so during the lead up to the full moon – live bait is best. When fishing from the pier, it is recommended that a surf rod be used, especially for these bigger species.

BAITS AND LURES

When searching for gummy sharks use fleshy baits or thick squid rings. Elephant fish will eat just about anything but half pilchards and squid are ideal. Mulloway are best targeted with live or fresh bait (caught that day). King George whiting are best fished for with squid and pipi.

BEST TIDE/TIMES

Two hours before high tide and an hour after is usually the prime time. The area becomes quite difficult to fish during the middle of the tide due to the strong current that exists. There is a sand bar directly opposite the pier. The further you cast, the shallower the water, so concentrate on casts of only 5 to 6 m to find the deeper water.

AMENITIES

There is a toilet block open to the public at the Caravan Park. There is also a general store near the end of Corinella Road.

KIDS AND FAMILIES

Corinella pier is a great place for the kids. The pier is well lit at night, wide and a hand rail features on one side.

FINALLY

There are plenty of fish to be caught with reasonable facilities within the immediate area. Concentrate on fishing the deep water in front of the pier for your chance to tangle with some big fish.

SEASONS

Gummy shark
Year round

Elephant fish
March to May

King George whiting
Summer

Mulloway
February to March

SETTLEMENT POINT

🔍 HOW TO GET THERE

Peter Street, Corinella. Follow the Bass Highway and turn right at Corinella Road. Turn left onto Smythe Street and follow this to the Corinella Foreshore Caravan Park. Park to the left of the Corinella Pier and you will see the rock platform to the west.

🔍 SNAPSHOT

PLATFORM
ROCK

TARGET FISH
SNAPPER
ELEPHANT SHARK
WHITING
GUMMY SHARK

BEST BAIT
CURED EEL
PIPI
MUSSEL
BABY BOTTLE SQUID
PILCHARD
SQUID

BEST LURES
SOFT PLASTIC WORMS
& GRUBS

BEST TIMES
LOW TIDE ONLY.

SEASONS

Snapper & whiting
Summer

Gummy shark
Year round

Elephant fish
March to May

Yellow-eye mullet
Year round

Mulloway
Summer

ocated to the far left of the Corinella Pier is Settlement Point – a rocky feature providing anglers with access to the channel during a low tide. This location is very rocky, but yields some amazing catches at times. While it is recommended that it is fished on a low tide, the water depth averages three metres. The rocks can be quite slippery due to the Neptune's Necklace seaweed that is present.

TACTICS

Throughout the summer months, particularly from September until November, snapper can be targeted from the rocks. Due to the heavy reef structure, paternoster rigs should be tied from 60 or 80 lb trace to withstand rubbing on the rocks. Hook size for snapper should be a 5/0 suicide or 6/0 circle. The most favoured baits are pilchards and squid although garfish also works very well. Gummy sharks are a common catch by those willing to put in the time required. Ideally, the prime to fish for them is from a mid-tide until the bottom of the low. Mulloway tend to be more active during the warmer months with February and March the better months to fish. The lead up to the full moon is a very productive time.

BAITS AND LURES

A large fillet of cured eel is fantastic when used for gummy sharks, as they love the oily smell and small fish find it nearly impossible to tear apart. Squid and pilchards work well for pinkie snapper while pipi will do the job on the King George whiting.

BEST TIDE/TIMES

Settlement Point is a low tide only proposition as the rocks are fully submerged once the tide fills.

AMENITIES

There is a small general store at the end of Corinella Road. The Caravan Park is located on the foreshore as are public toilets.

KIDS AND FAMILIES

The Corinella pier is a better option for the little ones.

FINALLY

An excellent alternative to Corinella Pier – especially during summer when the holiday makers arrive.

CORONET BAY

HOW TO GET THERE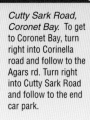

Cutty Sark Road, Coronet Bay. To get to Coronet Bay, turn right into Corinella road and follow to the Agars rd. Turn right into Cutty Sark Road and follow to the end car park.

SNAPSHOT

PLATFORM
BEACH

TARGET FISH
WHITING
PINKIE SNAPPER
CALAMARI
FLATHEAD

BEST BAIT
PIPI
BASS YABBIE
WHITEBAIT
PILCHARD
MUSSEL
BLUEBAIT

BEST LURES
SQUID JIGS

BEST TIMES
HIGH TIDE AT DAWN OR DUSK.

Coronet Bay is a unique landbased fishery. To the eye, this beach is not very appealing yet it produces some great catches of calamari, whiting, flathead and pinkie snapper. From the car park, the beach is quite shallow but on a low tide, you can wade out and cast into deeper water. There are plenty of weed beds where both squid and whiting are abundant. To the left heading towards the boat ramp an extensive reef system exists which holds some quality snapper and flathead in the warmer months. Anglers can also pump Bass yabbies at mid-tide to use for live baits when targeting whiting.

TACTICS
When the tide is low, wade out and cast as far as you possibly can. There are patches of weed and sand that make this location a very productive whiting fishery. The most successful technique is to use a paternoster rig tied from 15 lb trace with two droppers, each containing a single 1/0 circle hook or a size 6 long shank. Rock flathead can be specifically targeted by walking to the left towards the boat ramp and fishing amongst the reef. Here,

they lay in ambush for a meal. A running sinker rig tied from 15 lb trace with 2/0 suicide hook highly effective. Calamari can be caught in the same location but seem to prefer a baited jig rather than an artificial jig. Anglers seeking snapper will have to wade out amongst the reef where a long cast is required to access deeper water. Hook size may vary but a size 6/0 circle or 5/0 suicide will be adequate.

BAITS AND LURES
Whiting till take a variety of baits but pipi, squid strips and mussel all work considerably well. If you have a bait pump you can pump Bass yabbies from the mud flats. Pipi, pilchard, bluebait and whitebait are recommended and are rarely passed up. Artificial squid jigs are also very good when casting for calamari.

BEST TIDE/TIMES
The prime time to be fishing is first and last light during a high tide when the fish move into the shallower water to feed.

AMENITIES
There is a toilet block and playground located near the car park. A milk bar is accessible just up the main road.

KIDS AND FAMILIES
This beach is great to take children to but it is not recommended that you take them on the rocks as they are slippery.

FINALLY
This beach is a fantastic place to spend an evening on a hot night during a rising tide.

SEASONS

Squid
Summer

King George whiting
Summer

Pinkie snapper
Spring and summer

Flathead
Year round

KENNEDY POINT

🔍 HOW TO GET THERE

Bluff Road, Bass.
Follow Bass Highway and turn right into Soldiers Road and continue onto Bluff Road. There is parking close to the water.

🔍 SNAPSHOT

PLATFORM
BEACH

TARGET FISH
KING GEORGE
WHITING
LEATHERJACKET
SALMON
GUMMY SHARK

BEST BAIT
PIPI
MUSSEL
SQUID
CURED EEL
PILCHARD

BEST LURES
WORM STYLE SOFT
PLASTICS
BLADES

BEST TIMES
HIGH TIDE OR
SUNSET.

SEASONS

King George whiting
Summer – but winter produces bigger fish

Other species
Year round

To the eye, Kennedy Point isn't much to look at on arrival but yields some great fishing. The bottom is predominantly sand and gravel with few weed patches scattered throughout. This makes the perfect habitat for flathead. It is a relatively shallow beach that should be fished on the top of the high tide.

TACTICS

Anglers fishing from the bank can cast paternoster rigs with blue bait, white bait or pipi's and do very well. This area is quite shallow though and wading out to cast can be beneficial. Paternoster rigs should be tied from 10 to 12 lb trace with size 1/0 suicide hooks. Whiting are also a common catch on the high tide and can be caught using the same rigs as for flathead. Pipi's are the preferred bait, but mussels and live Bass yabbies also work well. A running sinker rig can also be used and should

be tied from 12 lb trace. The same hooks sizes should be used but if you're specifically targeting whiting then you should use a size 6 long shank style hook.

BAITS AND LURES

Pipi, mussel and squid strips are all effective on whiting. It pays to make up some berley to attract them to the immediate area. It is surprising to see that some very big fish get taken from this shallow area. It pays to cast out a heavier outfit with a gummy shark bait as they can frequent the area.

BEST TIDE/TIMES

High tide or after dark. If you can fish here when the two align you're in with the best shot.

AMENITIES

There are none. Kennedy Point is slightly off the beaten track, hence no facilities and small crowds.

KIDS AND FAMILIES

There are better places to take the little ones as there is no shelter available.

FINALLY

The best fishing spot is on the mainland, to the south of Reef Island. The bank is steeper here and the water is a lot deeper. Look for the old fence that runs into the water. There really is some great fishing to be had during the last of the flood tide.

BASS RIVER

HOW TO GET THERE

Bass Landing Road, Bass. Turn off the South Gippsland Highway at Bass Landing Road and follow this road until you reach the river.

SNAPSHOT

PLATFORM
ESTUARY

TARGET FISH
KING GEORGE
  WHITING
ESTUARY PERCH
SALMON
TREVALLY
MULLOWAY

BEST BAIT
SQUID
PIPI
LIVE MULLET/
  SALMON

BEST LURES
SHALLOW DIVING
  HARDBODIES
CRANKBAIT
SOFT PLASTIC
  GRUBS

BEST TIMES
TIDE CHANGES AND
  HIGH TIDE.

The Bass River is a very diverse stretch of water that runs from Poowong through to the township of Bass before emptying out into Western Port. The upper reaches contain freshwater and as such provide home to blackfish and trout. The lower stretch becomes estuarine and is home to a large variety of saltwater species.

TACTICS

Lure fishing works extremely well here. Most anglers prefer to use a light 2 to 5 kg graphite spin rod which can be held all day with ease. Braid is a must for repetitive and accurate casts towards the adjacent mangroves. If bait fishing, a paternoster rig will work well for most species and hooks should range from 2/0 to 4/0 for perch, flathead and salmon. Long shank hooks in size 10 are suitable for whiting and trevally while 6/0 snooded suicide hooks attached to an 80 lb leader is ideal when targeting mulloway. A running sinker rig, weighted as lightly as possible, is preferred for mulloway.

BAITS AND LURES

Small hardbody lures such as Owner Mira Shads and Yo-Zuri Alie Goby work particularly well. Your favourite soft plastics will come in handy too; try a scrub worm pattern if in doubt. Hop them across the bottom for flathead. Pipis and squid will work well for most species when bait fishing. If you can use fresh squid (caught that day) your success rate can double. Mulloway respond well to live baits such as salmon and mullet which are both available throughout the system.

BEST TIDE/TIMES

An hour each side of a tide change. High flood tides are also productive and worth prospecting.

AMENITIES

This location is slightly off the beaten track, which simply adds to the appeal for most.

There are no facilities nearby at all. The area is frequently closed due to irresponsible people failing to take rubbish home with them so remember to put all litter in a bag and discard of it thoughtfully.

KIDS AND FAMILIES

There are no facilities for children; however it is possible to fish close to the car park. It can be a little muddy near the water's edge so bring the gumboots but is otherwise safe.

FINALLY

The Bass River is both picturesque and productive. There are plenty of small fish to keep beginners and serious anglers entertained. Some nice whiting can be found close to the entrance on a tide change.

SEASONS

Most species will be in larger numbers around the summer months when water temperatures are up; however, it is a year-round fishery.

NEWHAVEN JETTY

🔍 HOW TO GET THERE

Beach Court, Newhaven. Go over the bridge onto Phillip Island. Turn right at the roundabout then right again into Beach Road. The jetty is about 500 m further along.

🔍 SNAPSHOT

PLATFORM
PIER

TARGET FISH
SILVER TREVALLY
AUSTRALIAN SALMON
GUMMY SHARK
YELLOW-EYE MULLET
SNAPPER

BEST BAIT
WHITEBAIT
PILCHARD
PIPI
SQUID HEADS
GARFISH
YELLOW-TAIL SCAD
SLIMY MACKEREL
CHICKEN FILLET

BEST LURES
BEST LURES
SOFT PLASTIC
WORMS
METAL LURES.

BEST TIMES
HIGH TIDE AT DAWN
AND DUSK.

SEASONS

Silver trevally
October to March

Australian salmon
Year round

Gummy shark
Summer

Yellow-eye mullet
Year round

Snapper
October to March

The Newhaven Pier is a very solid structure offering anglers a wide selection of fish to be caught from its end. It is situated within an easy cast of the channel in which anglers can access depths ranging 5 to 6 metres. The tide can run through here very fast making it very difficult throughout most of the tide. Ideally, the easiest and prime fishing times are at least two hours either side of a tide change.

TACTICS

Fishing two hours either side of the high tide change will be the most productive time for snapper as you can cast into the deeper water where they pass. A running sinker rig will work well as well as a paternoster rig. These rigs should be tied from at least 60 lb trace as there is some reef around that the snapper may run you over when hooked. Gummy sharks can be targeted in the same manner although it is suggested that the rig be upgraded to 80 pounds. Heavy sinkers and surf rods are required to hold bottom in the tide. Squid are abundant and are mostly caught during the night. Close to the start of the pier, the water can be calmer on the beginning of the run out tide.

BAITS AND LURES

A range of baits can be fished here depending on your target species. It pays to have a plan of attack here to ensure you have the right bait for the fish you're after. Squid and Bass yabbies are good for whiting whereas flesh baits are good for gummies and snapper. Squid jigs are best for the squid and pipi works well for mullet and trevally.

BEST TIDE/TIMES

Fishing one hour either side of the high tide is much more productive and easier due to less tidal movement. First and last light is best if the high tide coincides with this time.

AMENITIES

Toilets are located adjacent to the pier in the car park. There is also a supermarket 500 m away and a play area with BBQ facilities is close by.

KIDS AND FAMILIES

A safe location for kids, although strong currents make supervision a must. A beach area near the pier is handy for children to play.

FINALLY

A productive fishing location with a view of Western Port and the famous San Remo Bridge. Strong currents make fishing tough at times so focus your efforts around tide changes.

RHYLL JETTY

HOW TO GET THERE 🔍

Beach Road, Rhyll. The pier is located to the left at the end of Lock Road on Beach Road.

SNAPSHOT 🔍

PLATFORM
PIER

TARGET FISH
KING GEORGE WHITING
BAY TROUT
FLATHEAD
YELLOW-EYE MULLET

BEST BAIT
PIPI
BASS YABBIES
MUSSEL
SQUID STRIPS
PRAWN
PILCHARD FILLET
STIMULATE INSTANT BAIT

BEST LURES
SMALL METAL LURES
SOFT PLASTIC GRUBS AND MINNOWS

BEST TIMES
HIGH TIDE.

The Rhyll Jetty tends to get most attention during the summer months when anglers are on holidays on Phillip Island. The area surrounding the jetty is quite shallow with a depth around four meters. The bottom is mud yet is quite a good fishery for flathead and elephant sharks. A high tide is recommended when fishing.

TACTICS

Anglers fishing the bottom from the jetty catch most of the fish with a running sinker rig highly effective. This can be tied from 15 lb leader with 1/0 circle hooks ideal for all species. Due to the shallow water it is difficult to berley but it can still be achieved by sprinkling whole tuna oil soaked pellets into the water. By using this method, it will allow the pellets to rest on the bottom, where the tuna oil will attract fish to the area.

BAITS AND LURES

Whiting and flathead will take pipi baits and pilchard fillets. Small thin cut strips of squid are also an effective bait. When specifically targeting elephant fish, use half pilchards or squid strips and cast as far as you physically can to access the deeper water. Flathead can also be targeted with soft plastics.

BEST TIDE/TIMES

The incoming tide and top of the high tide is most productive. Morning and evening high tides will produce the best results.

AMENITIES

Within walking distance of the pier is the Rhyll Caravan Park and a service station which sells bait and fishing tackle, as well as snacks.

KIDS AND FAMILIES

A good place to take the kids who can play on surrounding grasslands and a playground nearby. Swimming is possible during the slack tide but supervision is required at all times.

FINALLY

During the holiday season Rhyll Pier is very popular. It pays to arrive early to get the best spots.

SEASONS

Yellow-eye mullet
Year round

Bay trout
Year round

Whiting
November to March

Flathead
Year round

SILVERLEAVES

🔍 HOW TO GET THERE

Silverleaves Beach is located on Phillip Island, east of Cowes. To get there from Phillip Island Rd turn right into Settlement Road and turn left into Coghlan Road. Follow to the end finding car parking where possible. This beach can be fished right where you access or to the far right.

🔍 SNAPSHOT

PLATFORM
BEACH

TARGET FISH
WHITING
FLATHEAD

BEST BAIT
ESTUARY WORMS
BASS YABBIES
PIPI
MUSSEL
BLUEBAIT

BEST LURES
WRIGGLER STYLE
SOFT PLASTICS

BEST TIMES
EVENING HIGH TIDE.

SEASONS

King George whiting
Summer

Flathead
Summer

Silverleaves is a beach that receives very little fishing pressure by landbased anglers but yields some amazing catches of whiting and flathead during the summer months.

TACTICS

Both whiting and flathead can be caught on the same rig with a paternoster being the most effective. This should be tied from either 8 or 10 lb leader with size 6 long shank hooks for whiting and 1/0 long shanks for flathead. On a warm summer's evening, you can often find flathead right up into the sand divots chasing baitfish. Light 7 ft 2 to 4 kg rods with 2500 series reel loaded with 6 lb braid suit very well for lure flicking and bait fishing. Ideally, when targeting whiting, an 8 or 9 ft light tapered spin rod works well. The tide strength doesn't affect the fishing here so you should be able to get away with size 1 to 3 oz bomb style sinkers.

BAITS AND LURES

Estuary worms and Bass yabbies can be pumped from the flats and make very good bait. Pipi, mussel and bluebait are also recommended. Anglers can also use lures to catch flathead in this area. Soft plastics work exceptionally well and should be used with a 1/8 oz jighead with a 2/0 hook. Squidgy fish and wriggler style plastics work quite well.

BEST TIDE/TIMES

A rising high tide after a hot day is very productive on dusk.

AMENITIES

The nearest amenities to this location are located in Cowes. There are plenty of shops, a toilet block and playground located on the Cowes foreshore.

KIDS AND FAMILIES

The location is a good place for children to play in the sand but it is away from most amenities. The currents are not a real concern on the sand flat, but can be if they stray into the deeper water.

FINALLY

If you're on holidays, this location is worth strolling to late in the evening. It can be very productive at times.

COWES PIER

HOW TO GET THERE 🔍

Phillip Island Road.
Cowes Pier is located
on the northern side
of Phillip Island. To
get there follow Phillip
Island road from San
Remo right to its end.
A car park is located at
the base of the pier.

SNAPSHOT 🔍

PLATFORM
PIER

TARGET FISH
SQUID
KING GEORGE
 WHITING
GUMMY SHARK
ELEPHANT FISH
FLATHEAD
AUSTRALIAN SALMON
TREVALLY
BARRACOUTA
SNAPPER
MULLET

BEST BAIT
SQUID
PILCHARD
CURED EEL
PIPI
WHITEBAIT
FISH FLESH

BEST LURES
SQUID JIGS
METAL SLUGS
A VARIETY OF SOFT
 PLASTICS

BEST TIMES
TWO HOURS EITHER
SIDE OF BOTH HIGH
AND LOW TIDES.

Located on Phillip Island's northern side, Cowes Pier becomes extremely popular with holiday makers during the summer months. The pier is very sturdy with few lower platforms allowing anglers to get closer to the water. The tide can run past the pier at a rate of knots and as such requires anglers to fish with sinkers up to eight ounces. Casting out from the end of the pier, you can expect to be fishing in depths ranging from 8 to 10 m of water. Practically every species found in Western Port can be caught from the Cowes Pier.

TACTICS
Elephant fish can be caught throughout the day/night on any tide. Elephants are generally caught when using a running sinker rig with 3/0 circle hook. Gummy sharks are also a highly prized catch and tend to be caught when anglers are using fresh baits such as trevally, salmon and tuna fillets. Gummies and snapper feed predominantly on the bottom where a running sinker rig works well. This should be tied from 80 lb trace with a 6/0 circle hook or 5/0 suicide hook attached. Artificial squid jigs are effective around the pier lights after dark and lures can be cast during the day for barracouta and salmon.

BAITS AND LURES
Fresh baits are best for snapper and gummy sharks. For best results use oily baits such as salmon and trevally fillets. Pilchards are also effective and are eaten by just about everything that swims in water. Metal lures and soft plastics can be cast for barracouta and salmon during the day. Pipi and squid are ideal for whiting and trevally and best fished on a paternoster rig with some red beads for extra attraction.

BEST TIDE/TIMES
A low tide early in the morning or on dusk is the prime time for targeting whiting.
Concentrate your efforts around two hours either side of a tide change for best results.
When targeting gummy sharks, fishing well into the night best produces quality fish.

AMENITIES
There are public toilet blocks located to the right and left of the pier. The foreshore reserve has play equipment and at the base of the pier is a small café. Shops can be found in the main street, 500 m from the pier.

KIDS AND FAMILIES
The foreshore reserve is nice and clean. If children are supervised, swimming in the shallows can be entertaining but beware, strong currents can exist very close to the shoreline.

FINALLY
During holiday periods this location is always happening, plenty to do and plenty to see. A good time can be had by all.

SEASONS
Squid, barracouta &
snapper
September to December

Whiting
November

Elephant fish
February to April

Australian salmon
January to April

Trevally
June to August

Others
Year round

RED ROCKS POINT

HOW TO GET THERE

Red Rocks Road, Ventnor. Turn right off Ventnor Road onto Red Rocks Road and continue to the end car park.

SNAPSHOT

PLATFORM
BEACH

TARGET FISH
ELEPHANT FISH
FLATHEAD
KING GEORGE
  WHITING
LEATHERJACKET
SQUID

BEST BAIT
PILCHARD
PRAWN
SQUID
WHITEBAIT
BLUEBAIT
PIPI

BEST LURES
SQUID JIGS

BEST TIMES
HIGH TIDE INTO
THE EVENING.

SEASONS

Elephant fish
Late March to early May

King George whiting
November to February

Others
Year round

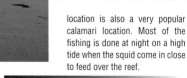

Located on the western side of Phillip Island, Red Rocks Point can become quite popular with anglers during the summer months in search of calamari and whiting. The area surrounding the point is quite reefy with plenty of weed growth and few sand patches. The depth ranges from 1 to 2 meters.

TACTICS

Fishing from Red Rocks Point will require anglers to hold their rods at all times as the fishing can be fast and furious. This is a whiting domain and when using pipi for bait, they can be quick to set upon it. There is no real need to cast far at this location as during a high tide whiting come in close to the reef. A paternoster rig suits very well but anglers will become snagged on occasion so it pays to have a few pre-rigged. A size 6 long shank hook will suit here as anglers will have to be at the ready feeling for the bite. From September until November, this location is also a very popular calamari location. Most of the fishing is done at night on a high tide when the squid come in close to feed over the reef.

BAITS AND LURES

Popular baits include squid, pilchard, prawn, bluebait, whitebait, silver whiting and pipis.

BEST TIDE/TIMES

For best results, fish an evening high tide until night fall.

AMENITIES

BBQ and picnic tables, grassland, gravel car park, rubbish bins, public toilets and good clear access paths to the beach.

KIDS AND FAMILIES

Red Rocks Point is an ideal location to take children fishing thanks to a sandy beach to play on as well as amenities nearby.

FINALLY

There is lots of room for fishing and good amenities with the BBQ being only a few metres away. Take the family, some food and make a day of it.

McHAFFIE POINT

HOW TO GET THERE

Grossard Point Road, Ventnor. McHaffie Point is located at the end of Grossard Point Road.

SNAPSHOT

PLATFORM
BEACH

TARGET FISH
GUMMY SHARK
SQUID
SNAPPER
FLATHEAD
KING GEORGE WHITING

BEST BAIT
PILCHARD
CURED EEL
SALMON FILLET
SQUID
SILVER WHITING
PIPI

BEST LURES
SOFT PLASTICS
METAL LURES

BEST TIMES
HIGH TIDE DURING LOW LIGHT PERIODS.

SEASONS

Gummy Sharks
Year round

Squid
Year round

Snapper
September to March

King George whiting
Summer

McHaffie Point is a top location where anglers can fish for a variety of species without having to cast long distances. Heavy reef surrounds the rocks with an average depth of three metres in close proximity. To the right of the rocks there is a large sand hole which holds good numbers of whiting and calamari in season. This is signified by a red marker buoy about 100 m out from the beach.

TACTICS

During the summer months, whiting are in abundance in the large sand hole to the right of the rocks. Fishing for them should be on a high tide when they are more likely to push into the shallower water. A paternoster rig will work well when tied from 10 lb fluorocarbon leader. Size 6 long shank hooks or Black Magic KL 1/0 hooks suit well. To fish for whiting, a light surf rod in a 10 to 11 ft length is recommended. This should be coupled with a 4000 series reel holding 300 m of 10 lb braid. With the large amount of weed beds and reef in the area, calamari are in abundance. The most effective method is to cast baited jigs with silver whiting under a float into the deeper water from the point.

BAITS AND LURES

Silver whiting works well on squid, while pipi and squid are best for whiting. On the slack tide, soft plastics can be hopped along the bottom for flathead. If you're a spinning enthusiast, pike and snook are a common catch. Arma Twist and Anchovy lures work very well when retrieved at a medium pace. A high tide is recommended.

BEST TIDE/TIMES

For gummy sharks, squid, snapper and whiting a high tide in the evening or after dark is recommended. A slack tide is best for casting soft plastics amongst the reef structure for flathead.

AMENITIES

There are no amenities within the immediate beach area; however there is a take away shop on Ventnor Road.

KIDS AND FAMILIES

Although the fishing platform is rocky, adjacent to it is a sandy beach and shallow water where children can play and swim.

FINALLY

McHaffie Point is a productive location to spend the night fishing. A variety of species can be targeted which can make it interesting too.

FLYNNS REEF

HOW TO GET THERE

Ventnor Road, Ventnor. After going through the roundabout at the Penguin Parade, turn right at the next roundabout and follow this road to the Flynns Reef car park.

SNAPSHOT

PLATFORM
BEACH

TARGET FISH
KING GEORGE
 WHITING
FLATHEAD
LEATHERJACKET
SNAPPER

BEST BAIT
PIPI
MUSSEL
PILCHARD
SQUID
PRAWN
BLUEBAIT
WHITEBAIT

BEST LURES
SOFT PLASTICS
BLADES

BEST TIMES
HIGH TIDE AT DUSK.

SEASONS

King George whiting
December to March

Others
Year round

Mainly a well-known surf break, Flynn's Reef can be a challenge to fish because of this reason. Despite this being the case, late evenings, night-time and early mornings are good times to fish here, especially on a rising tide. If you walk around the corner, there is a small sandy beach which anglers can target whiting. Casting from the sand, you will reach a depth of around 3 to 4 m of water. While there is some reef around, this location holds some very sizeable whiting throughout the year.

TACTICS

Flynn's Reef isn't the easiest location to fish but can be productive for whiting. This area is well-known for its winter whiting and can be extremely productive when fishing from the beach. Fishing in calm weather is more enjoyable with anglers required to cast as far as they physically can. In this case avoid fishing in strong southerlies or northerlies. Due to the reef, rigs will have to be tied from at least 20 lb fluorocarbon leader with size 4 long shank hooks. Either a paternoster or running sinker rig will suffice. Due to its location, it is suggested that either a 10 or 11 ft light to medium surf rod be used.

BAITS AND LURES

Pipi's are the preferred bait for most of the year but when it comes to winter whiting, use pilchard fillets.

BEST TIDE/TIMES

A high tide at dawn or dusk is best. On a low tide, casting further is very important to reach the deeper water where the fish are located.

AMENITIES

Located to the right of the sand path are public toilets and shops are located in either direction of Flynns Reef – at the Nobbies and on Ventnor Road.

KIDS AND FAMILIES

A good safe beach for children to play in the sand. Strong currents do exist but the beach itself is safe. A great location to take children fishing.

FINALLY

This beach can be very productive if fished during a rising tide. With a lot of room to fish it's a good location to fish during summer.

CAT BAY

HOW TO GET THERE

Ventnor Road, Summerlands. Follow Ventnor Road until you reach the car park which is 100 m on the right after the Penguin Parade roundabout.

SNAPSHOT

PLATFORM
BEACH

TARGET FISH
KING GEORGE
WHITING
SQUID
LEATHERJACKET

BEST BAIT
PIPI
MUSSEL
BASS YABBIES
FISH FILLETS
SILVER WHITING

BEST LURES
SQUID JIGS

BEST TIMES
INCOMING TIDE AND HIGH TIDE.

Cat Bay is one of the best landbased locations in Western Port as it supports a wide variety of species that can be caught. The beach is easy to reach and there are extensive reefs all within casting distance from the shore. The offshore swell can push in here making fishing difficult which is why it is more comfortable to fish it in an easterly or southerly wind. Its depth varies greatly but you'll mainly be casting into five metres of water.

TACTICS

Gummy sharks, seven gillers and bronze whalers are the most highly prized from this location and some fish can be huge. When fishing for these fish, heavy tackle is required. A running sinker rig will suffice but should be tied from 80 lb trace as the reef can damage or cut the line when the fish run. Hooks ranging from 6/0 to 8/0 are ideal. Calamari are also a worthy catch but a flat calm day is recommended to be fished. A paternoster rig suits this location when whiting fishing but you may also come into contact with pinkie snapper and leatherjackets. The rig should be tied from 15 lb fluorocarbon leader as a minimum. Hook choice is vital, use a circle hook for whiting and leatherjacket and a size 4/0 suicide for snapper.

BAITS AND LURES

All of these fish respond well to pipi, mussel, and Bass yabbies. When in search of calamari, silver whiting and squid jigs are the best option. Oily fish baits are ideal for sharks. Berley can be used here and it is best if discarded fish frames or old bait is placed into an onion bag and left to float around in the shore break.

BEST TIDE/TIMES

The incoming tide is best fished for whiting and leatherjacket, with a high tide at night for squid.

AMENITIES

Gravel car park, good access paths to the beach, public toilets and rubbish bins.

KIDS AND FAMILIES

A great place to take children. It is mostly sand with reef areas located about 15 m into the water. Strong currents are rarely found here but unexpected large waves can occur.

FINALLY

Likely to be filled with surfers, a little courtesy may be necessary. Try walking down the beach about 50 m or so to find better holes where fish are located – it's definitely worth it.

SEASONS

King George whiting
Winter for big whiting summer for numbers

Squid
Year round

Leatherjacket
Year round

Sharks
Year round – summer is peak.

COWRIE BEACH

HOW TO GET THERE

Ventnor Road, Summerlands. Follow Ventnor Road to the end car park.

SNAPSHOT

PLATFORM
ROCKS

TARGET FISH
SNAPPER
TREVALLY
GARFISH
SQUID
SHARKS
SALMON
KING GEORGE
  WHITING
BARRACOUTA
PIKE
MULLET
WRASSE

BEST BAIT
PILCHARD
SQUID
PRAWN
SILVERFISH
PIPI
WHITEBAIT
BLUEBAIT
SILVERFISH
MUSSEL
BASS YABBIES

BEST LURES
METAL LURES
SOFT PLASTIC
MINNOWS

BEST TIMES
AN EVENING HIGH
TIDE.

SEASONS

Snapper
November to March

Whiting
December to February

Trevally & salmon
Winter

Others
Year round

Cowrie Beach is a platform made of eroded basalt rock. At the water's edge it drops away to five meters where the bottom is mostly sand but also contains patches of reef. There are a few fingers of reef that stick out from which you can stand to get a further cast into the deeper water. Care must be taken on the rocks here. Cowrie Beach should not be fished in a westerly wind as the ocean swells can be treacherous.

TACTICS

Garfish are a common target along with calamari and whiting. Once you setup your post, be sure to scour the area to find a sandy patch where whiting can be found. To fish for whiting use a paternoster rig. With the area containing heavy reef patches, you may need to tie your rig from 20 lb leader. The current isn't too bad through here so you can get away with using a five ounce sinker most of the time but use lighter if possible. While calamari are available year round, the larger models can be caught in September/October. These can range from 2 to 3 kg and are primarily caught using a baited jig. Because you do have access right to the water's edge, you can flick artificial jigs around. Sharks do frequent the area so if you plan to target them use surf rods and 30 to 50 lb main line.

BAITS AND LURES

Pilchard, squid, bluebait, whitebait, prawn, pipi, silverfish, mussel and Bass yabbies will attract most species within the area. Bigger and oilier baits such as fish fillets, pilchards and whole squid can be used for snapper, gummies and sharks.

BEST TIDE/TIMES

A rising tide during the afternoon and into the evening is ideal.

AMENITIES

Shops, public toilets and a visitor centre are all nearby.

KIDS AND FAMILIES

With most of the fishing platforms made of uneven rocks, care must be taken and kids should not be taken here.

FINALLY

Cowrie beach is made up of a group of areas to fish rather than just one rock formation so there's plenty of room. Scope out the area at low tide to find the best looking areas to cast.

KITTY MILLER BAY

Kitty Miller Road, Ventnor. Kitty Miller Bay is located at the end of Kitty Miller Bay Road.

SNAPSHOT

PLATFORM
ROCK/BEACH

TARGET FISH
KING GEORGE WHITING
GARFISH
GUMMY SHARK
SALMON
LEATHERJACKET
TREVALLY
FLATHEAD

BEST BAIT
PIPI
SQUID
PEELED PRAWN
SLIVER FISH
BASS YABBIES
SALMON FILLET
EEL
MUSSEL

BEST LURES
MINNOW STYLE
SOFT PLASTICS
METAL LURES
BLADES

BEST TIMES
HIGH TIDE WILL PRODUCE THE BEST CATCH.

SEASONS

King George whiting
November to February

Trevally
Summer months

Salmon
Winter months

Others
Year round

Kitty Miller Bay is a very reefy location that can be difficult to fish. Often, it takes its toll on anglers tackle boxes due to the amount of tackle lost. While the beach itself looks fishable enough, it isn't. There is a walking track to the right of the beach which takes you to a series of basalt fingers which jut out into Bass Strait. The first finger is the prime fishing location, where a good cast will access some sandy bottom. The depth ranges from 3 to 5 metres.

TACTICS

Though Kitty Miller Bay is a very reefy location, many species of wrasse and leatherjackets can be caught. Garfish are also plentiful along with whiting if you cast to the sand patches. Anglers fishing from the rocks are advised to use berley to attract fish in close. If you're fishing the bottom for whiting, a paternoster rig works very well, though it needs to be tied from 20 lb trace for abrasion resistance against the rocks. Ideal hooks are a long shank size 6 or Black Magic 1/0 KL circle.

BAITS AND LURES

Pipi, peeled prawn, Bass yabbies, squid strips, and mussel are all effective on whiting, while salmon and eel fillet are best for gummy sharks. Soft plastic jerk shads and grubs are perfect for the flathead and garfish respond well to silverfish.

BEST TIDE/TIMES

Check out the area on a low tide to help locate the main rock structure points and to get a good understanding of the terrain. On the high tide, fishing for whiting produces good results in the bay type area as they move into the shallows to feed. For all other species, fishing from the rock wall is a prime location on an evening high tide. Swell height and wind direction will need to be taken into consideration before fishing the rock platform.

AMENITIES

There are no amenities within the immediate area.

KIDS AND FAMILIES

Most suitable for children to play on the sand, but the rocks are slippery on the low tide and supervision is a must. At high tide the rocks are completely immersed.

FINALLY

This location is not often spoken about, mainly because the locals know it's a good thing. Watch where the locals fish on a high tide and follow suit for best results.

BERRY'S BEACH

HOW TO GET THERE

Berry's Beach Road, Ventnor. From Back Beach Road which runs almost the length of the island, take the Berry's Beach Road turn off and follow to the end where there is a gravel car park.

SNAPSHOT

PLATFORM
ROCK

TARGET FISH
KING GEORGE
  WHITING
LEATHERJACKET
FLATHEAD

BEST BAIT
PIPI
BASS YABBIES
MUSSEL
PRAWN
WHITEBAIT
BLUEBAIT

BEST LURES
SOFT PLASTIC GRUBS
  AND PADDLE TAILS

BEST TIMES
HIGH TIDE IN THE
  EVENING.

SEASONS

King George whiting
November to February

Leatherjacket
Summer months

Flathead
Year round

Tiger flathead
Throughout summer

Garfish
Summer

Berry's Beach receives very little fishing pressure due to its location but it can produce some memorable catches. The beach is very reefy with plenty of rock features lying beneath the surface. Along both sides of the beach there are basalt rocks and boulders. Although it can be difficult to find a place to fish without becoming snagged this location does have a little gem about it. For one reason or another this beach attracts some monster garfish and ocean whiting throughout the year.

TACTICS
The most effective time to fish this location is during a northerly wind. A northerly will blow the waves flat, keeping the area relatively calm. When conditions are right garfish swarm the area and are great fun to catch. To be successful on garfish, a berley trail needs to be established. A float rig is recommended with slightly larger hooks such as size 10 due to the size of the garfish that can be caught. A paternoster rig will suit for whiting but keep things as light as possible. A suggestion is tying the rig from 8 or 10 lb leader with two size 6 long shank hooks or Black Magic KL 1/0 circle hooks.

BAITS AND LURES
Best baits for whiting include Bass yabbies, pipi, mussel and prawn. For garfish try silverfish, pipi pieces and slithers of pilchard. Soft plastics in various patterns work well on flathead.

BEST TIDE/TIMES
An early morning high tide is most productive here. Fish during overcast days for best results.

AMENITIES
Gravel car park.

KIDS AND FAMILIES
A soft sandy beach will keep kids entertained however they must be supervised due to strong currents and wave activity.

FINALLY
A quiet fishing location year round that can produce some great fishing. Care must be taken when rock fishing; so never turn your back on the waves.

CUNNINGHAM BAY

HOW TO GET THERE

Gap Road, Ventnor.
Follow Back Beach Road and turn left into Gap Road just before the Phillip Island race track. Continue to the end car park.

SNAPSHOT

PLATFORM
ROCKS

TARGET FISH
TREVALLY
SWEEP
AUSTRALIAN SALMON
WRASSE
SNAPPER
FLATHEAD

BEST BAIT
PIPI
BLUEBAIT
WHITEBAIT
PILCHARD FILLET
BASS YABBIES
PEELED PRAWN

BEST LURES
METAL SLUGS
HEAVIER SQUID JIGS
SOFT PLASTIC GRUBS AND CURL TAIL WORMS

BEST TIMES
LOW TIDE.

SEASONS

Trevally
September to November

Whiting
November to February

Others
Year round

Cunningham Bay is a location not for the faint-hearted. Located behind the Phillip Island race track, the walk in is very difficult. A small, partly worn dirt track weaves down the hill which can be difficult to navigate with a load of gear and tackle. The fishing platform is the rocks right in front of the path down. The rocks are basalt and uneven, making walking difficult and care must be taken. The depth is around four meters and contains reef and sand patches.

TACTICS

The main targeted species here is both silver trevally and whiting although calamari are also a possible target. Cast a baited jig under a float for best results. Silver trevally can be attracted to the area using berley which is extremely effective. From the rocks, berleying is best employed with an onion bag which can be lowered into the water near the rocks. Silver trevally have only a small mouth so hooks need to be a long shank size 6 or similar. These should be attached to a paternoster rig tied from 15 lb trace. When using this rig, whiting will also be caught. Due to the wave action, sinkers in the 4 to 6 oz range

may be required. As such, surf rods are ideal as is a backpack with limited gear.

BAITS AND LURES

Pilchard, bluebait, squid, Bass yabbies, pipis and peeled prawn are all good options at this location. Peeled prawn seems to be a stand out bait here.

BEST TIDE/TIMES

Low tide is the easiest, but you will have to walk to the edge of the rocks (which can be fished throughout the entire tide cycle). High tide can be fished but you'll lose a lot of gear amongst the submerged rocks.

AMENITIES

There are no amenities nearby.

KIDS AND FAMILIES

Not a chance. The walk down to the rock platform is hard enough for adults.

FINALLY

The rock platform can be a dangerous place to fish so ensure you check conditions before attempting to fish here. Northerly winds and small swells are the only times to fish.

HOW TO GET THERE

Woolamai Beach Road, Cape Woolamai. Turn left into Woolamai Beach Road from Phillip Island Road. Anzacs Beach and Cape Woolamai Surf Beach both have adequate car parking with public toilets and good wooden stairways providing access to the beach.

SNAPSHOT

PLATFORM
SURF

TARGET FISH
AUSTRALIAN SALMON
YELLOW-EYE MULLET
SILVER TREVALLY

BEST BAIT
PIPI
MUSSEL
BASS YABBIES
PILCHARD FILLET
BLUEBAIT
WHITEBAIT

BEST LURES
SURF POPPERS
SOFT PLASTICS
METAL LURES

BEST TIMES
HIGH TIDE, DAWN
AND DUSK.

SEASONS

Australian salmon
April to August

Yellow-eye mullet
Year round

Snapper
Autumn

Located on Phillip Island, Anzacs and Cape Woolamai Surf Beaches are extremely popular surf fishing locations during the winter months. This section of coastline is predominantly sand with a light gravel bottom in some of the gutters. These gravel areas tend to create deeper gutters compared to those of just sand and subsequently hold more fish. While salmon are the main catch, yellow-eye mullet and the odd snapper are also caught.

TACTICS

There are two main gutters to fish for salmon at Anzacs Beach: one is located approximately 200 m to the right of the stairs and contains the gravel bottom while to the left of the stairs, another gutter which is sand can be distinguished between the breaking swells. At Cape Woolamai surf beach there are a series of gutters spread right along the beach both to the left and right. Berley is essential to attract fish and can be setup with pellets, mashed pilchards and tuna oil all placed together in an onion bag. Salmon are best targeted with a paternoster rig with a 1/0 hook placed on the top dropper and a surf popper on the bottom. Although snapper aren't a common catch they are still possible during autumn. The gutter to the right containing the gravel bed is where they are mostly caught. Surf fishing requires the use of heavy tackle due to the strong currents and big waves that exist. Rods in the 12 ft range are suitable and depending on the sinker weights required on any given day the line rating will vary. Depending on the strength of the side wash, a 6 oz star sinker may be required but it

pays to have a selection ranging from 4 to 6 ounces. Traditionally, oversized reels holding 300 m of 25 lb monofilament were standard when it came to surf fishing but with the introduction of braided lines and better quality rods, the need for such heavy gear is no longer. Ideally, a 6000 or 8000 series reel loaded with 10 to 15 lb braid will do the job.

BAITS AND LURES
When fishing for salmon use bluebait, squid, whitebait and pipi on the top hook of a paternoster rig and a surf popper on the bottom. If you prefer to fish with lures use a 9 to10 ft rod for casting metal lures. Mullet respond well to small pipi and chicken baits.

BEST TIDE/TIMES
The run in tide is most productive, especially if you can align it with dawn or dusk. Overcast days are also more consistent than sunny days as they provide the fish with cover.

AMENITIES
Public toilets are located at the car park as well as at the surf life saving club at Cape Woolamai Surf Beach. A take away food shop can be found 5 minutes away near Cleeland Bight on Cottosloe Avenue.

KIDS AND FAMILIES
The beaches are great for kids as they offer plenty of sand for them to run around on. Unexpected waves are a possibility and strong currents exist so please supervise them at all times.

FINALLY
The two beaches provide excellent surf fishing options with easy access to the beach and shops. The best part is – neither beach becomes overcrowded with anglers even during the holiday season. Surfers are about in numbers though so be mindful of them.

MAGIC LANDS

HOW TO GET THERE

Woolamai Beach Road, Cape Woolamai. After going over the San Remo Bridge to Phillip Island, turn left into Cape Woolamai Road and drive to the end car park.

SNAPSHOT

PLATFORM
ROCK/BEACH

TARGET FISH
SHARKS
AUSTRALIAN SALMON
WRASSE
SNAPPER

BEST BAIT
WHOLE TUNA
SQUID
SLIMY MACKEREL
SALMON
MULLET FILLET

BEST LURES
METAL LURES
SURF POPPERS

BEST TIMES
INCOMING TIDE
UNTIL TOP OF
HIGH TIDE.

required. Baits need to be ballooned out where the wind and tide will carry it out into deeper water.

BAITS AND LURES

Big oily baits such as tuna, salmon and mackerel are recommended for sharks. Pilchard, bluebait, surf poppers and metal slugs will all produce salmon

BEST TIDE/TIMES

A full run-in tide is best, as fish move in closer to search for food in the gutters.

Offshore winds will aid in getting big baits and balloons out.

AMENITIES

Located at the Cape Woolamai car park are toilet facilities, a surf life saving club and clear access paths. Shops and cafés can be found as you turn into Cape Woolamai Road.

KIDS AND FAMILIES

Not suitable for children unless they remained on the nearby sand while under supervision.

FINALLY

Magic Lands is a popular with landbased game fishermen for big sharks and for good reason too. If you're dedicated to the cause then this may be the location you've been looking for.

Magic Lands isn't for the faint hearted as the walk in is quite lengthy along the beach. Access is from the Cape Woolamai car park to the left of the beach right down to the rocks. This area is quite deep and contains a lot of rocks on the bottom. In heavy seas this location can be difficult to fish but still yields a great catch.

TACTICS

Due to the rocks on the bottom, anglers should fish a paternoster rig tied from 20 lb trace. This should be used with a spoon sinker to prevent becoming snagged on the bottom. Salmon hooks can differ but a suicide size 3/0 or long shank size 1/0 is ideal. Salmon will respond well to most baits with bluebait, whitebait and pipi favourite choices. Larger sharks such as seven gillers can also be targeted from this location. It isn't easy though as you'll require the wind and tide to be in your favour. Ideally, to do this style of fishing, a northerly wind and a high tide is

SEASONS

Sharks
December to February for best numbers of fish

Salmon
Winter months

Others
Year round

RED POINT

🔍 HOW TO GET THERE

Cleeland Bight, Cape Woolamai. Take Woolamai Beach Road to the end car park, 200 m before the car park is a walking track. Follow this to the beach, turn right, and head to the rocky outcrop.

🔍 SNAPSHOT

PLATFORM
ROCK/BEACH

TARGET FISH
SNAPPER
AUSTRALIAN SALMON
BARRACOUTA
PIKE
WRASSE
GARFISH
LEATHERJACKET
KING GEORGE
WHITING

BEST BAIT
SQUID
PILCHARD
SAURIES
PIPI
BLUEBAIT
WHITEBAIT

BEST LURES
SOFT PLASTICS
METAL LURES
SQUID JIGS

BEST TIMES
BOTH HIGH AND LOW TIDES. RATHER THAN TRYING TO CAST A MILE, CONCENTRATE YOUR EFFORTS CLOSE TO THE ROCK STRUCTURE AS MANY FISH CAN BE FOUND HIDING NEARBY.

SEASONS

Snapper
November to March

Australian salmon
April to August

Others
Year round

R ed Point is one of the most productive landbased fishing locations for snapper in Western Port so it is certainly worth the walk. Located at the tip of Cape Woolamai on the eastern side, it provides anglers with access to the mouth of the Eastern Entrance where it meets Bass Strait. From the rocks anglers can cast into the mouth to fish the bottom where it is approximately eight metres deep. Light winds and small swells provide the most comfortable and safest conditions at this location.

TACTICS
Close into the rocks, calamari can be caught year round while a cast made into the blue can see whiting, flathead, snapper and gummy sharks caught off the bottom. Lure fishing is also effective for those flicking metal slugs in the 50 g range. This tends to attract barracouta, pike and snook although during the summer months, the odd kingfish can be hooked. From September through to December it is very common to catch snapper from this point although a lot of time and preparation needs to be put in to be successful. Some fish caught here have been weighed at a staggering eight kilograms which is a very respectable fish from the stones. Paternoster rigs and or running sinker rigs tied from 60 lb trace are recommended, as you may also hook gummy sharks.

BAITS AND LURES
Squid is effective for most species encountered here but try whole fish baits for your best chance of snaring a snapper. Metal lures and soft plastics can also be used on a range of species such as salmon, pike and flathead. Squid jigs and/or silver whiting presented under a float are also worth a shot for the local squid here.

BEST TIDE/TIMES
Both tides will produce fish so it's worth fishing here whenever conditions are safe enough to do so.

AMENITIES
There are no amenities in the immediate area.

KIDS AND FAMILIES
Not suitable for children as it takes a long walk to get here.

FINALLY
Red Point is one of the best landbased locations in the port and well worth the effort to get to. Due to the long walking distance required to get to Red Point, anglers are reminded to limit their gear and take only the necessities.

CLEELAND BIGHT

HOW TO GET THERE

The Esplanade,
Cape Woolamai.
From Woolamai Beach
Road take the last left
into The Cranny and
follow to the car park.

SNAPSHOT

PLATFORM
BEACH

TARGET FISH
SQUID
SNAPPER
AUSTRALIAN SALMON
BARRACOUTA
LEATHERJACKET
FLATHEAD
KING GEORGE WHITING

BEST BAIT
SILVER WHITING
UNDER A FLOAT
SOFT PLASTICS
PILCHARD
PIPI
BLUEBAIT
SALTWATER FLIES
SOFT PLASTICS

BEST LURES
SOFT PLASTICS IN A
RANGE OF STYLES
SQUID JIGS
METAL SLUGS

BEST TIMES
HIGH TIDE WITH AN
EVENING TIDE
CHANGE.

SEASONS

Squid
September to November

Snapper
**Early season snapper
around September to
November**

Salmon
Winter

Barracouta
Year round

King George whiting
November to February

Others
Year round

Cleeland Bight is a sandy beach spanning approximately one kilometre. This area opens into Bass Strait, constantly getting a fresh flush of fresh ocean water. Within casting distance from the shore, the bottom is quite thick with sea grasses which provide cover for a wide range of species. On a high tide, the depth is around 4 to 5 m while on the low it drops to 2 or 3 metres.

TACTICS

Cleeland Bight is a productive beach for calamari amongst a plethora of others. The prime time is the high tide when fish will move closer in towards the beach and weed beds. A silver whiting suspended under a prong is the best method. Whiting can also be targeted from here on the low tide. There is some big whiting here and it is recommended a paternoster rig tied from 15 lb trace be used. Hook choice is critical as you'll have to bring the fish back over the weed where they can become snagged. A Black Magic KL 1/0 hook works really well in this situation. If you're up for a walk, you can head to the right of Cleeland Bight. There is a huge sand dune on the beach which children slide down. From here, you have good access to deep water where pinkie snapper can be caught along with whiting. When fishing this location a long surf rod is required.

BAITS AND LURES

Pilchard and bluebait are most productive for flathead, while pipi and squid are best for whiting. Soft plastics are extremely effective on a range of species here – especially at low tide. Take a range of styles and colours and persist with various retrieves.

BEST TIDE/TIMES

Check the beach out at low tide to get a better understanding of its make-up. During the high tide it looks like a sandy beach. On low tide the reef is exposed and this is when anglers can search for the most productive area to be fished.

AMENITIES

Car park, public toilets, sandy beaches and nearby milk bar.

KIDS AND FAMILIES

A great place to take kids and families. The sand offers a safe area for children to play and the shallows are safe to swim in when supervised. Strong currents exist further out so don't head out deep.

FINALLY

A pleasant place to fish with friends and family and a great place to catch a feed.

SAN REMO JETTY

Marine Parade, San Remo. Just before driving onto the bridge from San Remo to Phillip Island, turn left into the shops and follow the road to the pier.

SNAPSHOT

PLATFORM
BEACH

TARGET FISH
KING GEORGE
  WHITING
SQUID
LEATHERJACKET
BARRACOUTA
SNAPPER

BEST BAIT
PIPI
PEELED PRAWN
PILCHARD FILLET
SILVER WHITING
SAURIES
SQUID
EEL
FRESH FISH FILLETS

BEST LURES
METAL SLUGS
MINNOW STYLE
  SOFT PLASTICS

BEST TIMES
SLACK WATER, LAST
  HOUR OF HIGH AND
  LOW TIDE.

SEASONS

King George whiting
**Late November to
February**

Squid
Year round

Snapper
November to February

Barracouta
November to December

Leatherjacket
Year round

The San Remo Pier is located to the left, just before the bridge that leads to Phillip Island. It is used to house the trawler boats and as such is quite picturesque and popular. It varies in depths ranging from 5 to 10 m and the bottom is sandy with patches of reef and a deep channel runs directly in front of the pier. The current runs extremely fast through here so heavy sinkers are required to fish the entire tide.

TACTICS
Surf rods are suitable here due to the heavier sinkers required; however lighter tackle can be used when fishing an hour either side of the tide change. The paternoster rig is versatile and effective here but employ a running or fixed sinker rig when chasing snapper. Use silver whiting under a float an hour before the slack tide and an hour after for your best chance of encountering big squid. Barracouta are best targeted with metal lures or minnow style soft plastics cranked back at a steady pace.

BAITS AND LURES
Pilchard, pipi, peeled prawn, sauries and squid are good for most species. Silver whiting is dynamite for catching calamari when using a prong under a float; however, artificial jigs are also productive.

Gummy sharks will take fish fillets, eel chunks and tuna strips. Lures are best for barracouta but watch out for their teeth if you do land one.

BEST TIDE/TIMES
For all species except squid, the last hour of the run-out tide and first hour of the run-in tide are best. When targeting squid, the slack water produces excellent results.

AMENITIES
There is a foreshore reserve to the right of the pier. BBQ facilities, public toilets, shops, cafés, car parks, fresh fish co-op (incase you end up empty-handed) and a tackle shop are within walking distance of the pier. Fresh bait can also be purchased from the local tackle shop.

KIDS AND FAMILIES
San Remo is an excellent location to take children. Apart from the fishing, the nearby foreshore has a playground, shops and many other child-friendly facilities. The kids might like to take some bread to feed the local birds.

FINALLY
The water flows extremely fast through here, and heavier sinkers are required to hold bottom. Time sessions around the tide change for best results.

KILCUNDA SURF BEACH

HOW TO GET THERE

Bass Highway, Kilcunda. After passing the Kilcunda shops you will drive past the Trestle Bridge on the right, approximately 100 m after the bridge there is a tar side road on the right. Turn into it and follow to the car park.

SNAPSHOT

PLATFORM
SURF/ROCK

TARGET FISH
AUSTRALIAN SALMON
YELLOW-EYE MULLET
SILVER TREVALLY
SNAPPER

BEST BAIT
PIPI
PILCHARDS
SQUID
BLUEBAIT
WHITEBAIT
SQUID
TUNA FILLETS

BEST LURES
METAL LURES
SURF POPPERS
SOFT PLASTICS

BEST TIMES
HIGH TIDE.

Kilcunda Surf Beach is the most popular surf fishing beach along the Bass Coast. Kilcunda is mostly a sandy beach with a rocky outcrop located to the right which also attracts some good fish due to the deeper water. There is a series of gutters all worthy of fishing but it pays to get there early before the beach is full of keen anglers. There is a deep gutter located just before the rocks to the right of the beach. During a strong wind blow, salmon often school up here in excellent numbers. This beach is best fished on a rising tide.

TACTICS
Salmon are the main targeted species and are mainly caught during the winter months. These fish can be caught to 3 kg and should be targeted with 20 lb paternoster rigs. A size 1/0 long shank or 2/0 bait holder hook works well. Gummy sharks should be targeted using a running or fixed sinker rig tied from 80 lb trace. A single Black 6/0 circle or twin snelled 5/0 suicide hooks work well. Surf rods work

extremely well here for all species. These should be at least 12 ft in length to combat large waves and strong side wash. Reels should be spooled with 20 to 30 lb braid to aid in winding big fish back up the beach.

BAITS AND LURES
A favourite bait for salmon is bluebait and whitebait but pipi's are worthy of being used.

BEST TIDE/TIMES
This beach is best fished on a rising tide. If fishing from the rocks make sure the swell is low and fish the first two hours of the run out tide. Do not fish the rocks in a south west or westerly wind, it can be dangerous.

AMENITIES
There are no amenities in the immediate area. Public toilets can be found at the foreshore reserve near the Kilcunda Caravan Park.

KIDS AND FAMILIES
Kilcunda is a popular beach amongst both families and anglers. Although it is quite a good location to take kids to the beach big swells are common so they must be supervised at all times.

FINALLY
This beach is very productive for salmon during winter and there is plenty of room to accommodate a number of anglers.

SEASONS
Australian salmon
April to August

Yellow-eye mullet
Year round

Silver trevally
November to December

CEMETERY BEACH

🔍 HOW TO GET THERE

Bass Highway, Kilcunda.
Approximately 100 m after the turn off for the Kilcunda Beach car park is a dirt road which enters the Cemetery on the right. Turn into it and follow around to the left where it enters a gravel car park. Follow the path to the beach.

🔍 SNAPSHOT

PLATFORM
SURF

TARGET FISH
AUSTRALIAN SALMON
SILVER TREVALLY
GUMMY SHARK
YELLOW-EYE MULLET

BEST BAIT
PIPI
MUSSEL
PILCHARD
SQUID
BLUEBAIT
WHITEBAIT
CURED EEL
FISH FILLETS

BEST LURES
METAL SLUGS
SURF POPPERS
SOFT PLASTIC
MINNOWS

BEST TIMES
TWO HOURS EITHER SIDE OF HIGH TIDE. NIGHT TIME FOR GUMMY SHARKS.

SEASONS

Australian salmon
April to August

Silver trevally
April to August

Gummy shark
Year round

Yellow-eye mullet
Year round

Hidden away from most beach goers, Cemetery Beach is very popular with anglers during the winter months. There are two main gutters, one to the left of the sand track and one to the right. Both are quite deep and hold good numbers of salmon. After a westerly blow, this beach can become weedy and prove a challenge to land fish.

TACTICS

One of the most effective techniques is to use berley in order to attract salmon and mullet to your chosen gutter. Berleying in the surf is as simple as filling an onion bag with pellets soaked in tuna oil and securing it to a rod holder. As the waves wash up the beach and flow over the onion bag they retreat, taking the berley back into the gutter. Over a short period of time, this will bring fish to the area. A paternoster rig works well with either two hooks or one hook and a surf popper. Suitable hooks are a 1/0 long shank or bait holder. The rig should be tied from at least 15 lb leader. Salmon respond well to bluebait, whitebait and pipi. If you choose not to berley it may pay to move from gutter to gutter or cast lures to help find the school. Often one piece of bait cast out won't attract a lot of fish and you may have to cover ground to locate a school of fish.

BAITS AND LURES

When fishing for salmon try using pipi, pilchard, bluebait, or whitebait. Lures such as soft plastics, surf poppers or metal slugs can also be used. Surf poppers laced with a small piece of squid or pipi do well. Gummy sharks are often caught when using cured eel, trevally fillet, salmon fillet, tuna fillet or fresh calamari.

BEST TIDE/TIMES

Fishing the high tide is necessary for all species. A high tide during the night is prime time if you want to target gummy sharks.

AMENITIES

Public toilets and a picnic area.

KIDS AND FAMILIES

Cemetery beach is O.K for children as they can play in the sand but swimming is out of the question due to large swells. This beach is quite secluded making it a great location to take the family.

FINALLY

As with most surf beaches Cemetery beach is productive for salmon if the right techniques are employed. Use plenty of berley and the fish will find your baits soon enough.

POWLETT RIVER

HOW TO GET THERE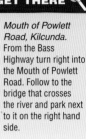

Mouth of Powlett Road, Kilcunda. From the Bass Highway turn right into the Mouth of Powlett Road. Follow to the bridge that crosses the river and park next to it on the right hand side.

SNAPSHOT

PLATFORM
ESTUARY

TARGET FISH
ESTUARY PERCH
BREAM
AUSTRALIAN
  SALMON
SILVER TREVALLY

BEST BAIT
BASS YABBIES
FRESHWATER
  YABBIES
SAND WORM
PIPI
PILCHARD FILLET
PRAWNS

BEST LURES
SOFT PLASTIC
  GRUBS AND
  WRIGGLERS
VIBES
SURFACE POPPERS
SHALLOW DIVING
  HARDBODIES

BEST TIMES
HIGH TIDE WHEN
  THE MOUTH IS
  OPEN.

The Powlett River is a unique estuary system that is quite small but can boast some fantastic fishing in the warmer months. The river is very shallow reaching a maximum of 1.5 m in parts and is very muddy with a few scattered weed beds about. The Powlett River is a fragile fishery that must be looked after. Despite being a small system – black bream, estuary perch and yellow-eye mullet can all be found. Small silver trevally and salmon can be caught but don't reach legal size limit.

TACTICS

Anglers wanting to target bream can do so by walking the river casting soft plastics, hard body lures and metal vibes. Most of the fish tend to inhabit the weed beds although; they can often be targeted around the bridge pylons. The most successful lures are the squidgy bloodworm wriggler in the 80 mm size, Instinct's Piccola, Ecogear SX 40's and similar style hardbody lures. Estuary perch are also a common catch using the same techniques as for bream. These fish are most active during the summer months with a warm night the prime time

to target them with small surface poppers. Lure fishing requires light tackle such as a 7 ft 2 to 4 kg rod with 2500 series reel and 6 lb braid.

BAITS AND LURES

Bream and perch respond well to a range of soft plastic and hardbody lures. Popular soft plastic patters include wrigglers, creature baits and grubs. Effective hardbodies include Ecogear VX 35, SX40, Min Min's and River 2 Sea Baby Vibes. Best baits include live Bass yabbies, freshwater yabbies, sand worm, pipi, pilchard fillet and prawns.

BEST TIDE/TIMES

Summer is quite productive for perch although they are still caught year round. Bream are much the same but are often in a feeding frenzy when there's a storm approaching. Salmon and trevally can be taken at any time. If the mouth is open fishing the high tide will be the most productive time.

AMENITIES

There are no amenities in the area.

KIDS AND FAMILIES

A great location to take the kids. The edges of the river can be very slippery so take some gumboots. If bait fishing they can sit on the side of the river and will have a great time catching plenty of fish.

FINALLY

A great location for the family to enjoy a peaceful day out. There isn't much else to do but you can have lots of fun exploring the area.

SEASONS

Estuary perch
Summer months

Bream
Year round

Australian salmon
Year round

Silver trevally
Year round

WILLIAMSONS BEACH

HOW TO GET THERE

Lower Powlett Road, Wonthaggi. Follow the Bass Highway through Kilcunda towards Wonthaggi. Directly opposite the Toyota dealership before the town, turn right into Lower Powlett Road. Follow this until you reach the car park.

SNAPSHOT

PLATFORM
SURF

TARGET FISH
AUSTRALIAN
AUSTRALIAN
  SALMON
YELLOW-EYE MULLET
GUMMY SHARK
SILVER TREVALLY

BEST BAIT
PIPI
MUSSEL
SQUID
PILCHARD
BLUEBAIT
WHITEBAIT
EEL FILLET
PILCHARDS
SALMONJ
TUNA AND TREVALLY
  FILLET

BEST LURES
SURF POPPERS
METAL SLUGS
MINNOW STYLE SOFT
  PLASTICS

BEST TIMES
HIGH TIDE FOR
SALMON AND
TREVALLY. LOW TIDE
FOR MULLET.

SEASONS

Australian salmon
April to August

Yellow-eye mullet
Year round

Silver trevally
April to August

Williamson's is a long stretch of beach approximately five kilometres long. It features a lot of deep and fishable gutters with the two most prominent in close proximity to the walking track. It is one of the deepest beaches along this coast with an average of three metres depth spanning the entire beach. The most productive gutter is the one located 70 m to the left of the walking path.

TACTICS

Surf rods are required at this location unless you're into casting lures whereby a 10 ft casting rod is recommended. The most useful rig is a two dropper paternoster tied from 16 to 20 lb leader. Unless there is strong side drift, stick with a 4 oz star sinkers. Hooks for salmon should be a 1/0 bait holder and size 10 long shank for mullet and silver trevally. Surf poppers in blue/white or red/white are very popular when tied onto the bottom dropper of the paternoster rig. Some soft pastics can also be used as a substitute for a surf popper. Salmon will take metal slugs and anglers should cast and retrieve them in a gutter or through a berley trail for best results.

BAITS AND LURES

Bluebait, whitebait, pipi and pilchards are ideal to use for salmon. Mullet and trevally are often taken when using pipi and mussel baits although small fillets of pilchard work well. Lure anglers can also catch their fair share of fish while casting metal slugs and retrieving at high speed. Instead of fishing two baits on a paternoster rig, surf poppers or soft plastics can be threaded on the bottom dropper.

BEST TIDE/TIMES

Two hours either side of the high tide for salmon and silver trevally. Fishing an hour either side of the low tide change is most productive for yellow-eye mullet.

AMENITIES

There are no amenities in the immediate area. Shops and public toilets can be found in the town of Wonthaggi, a 5 to 10 minute drive from Williamsons Beach.

KIDS AND FAMILIES

This is a great beach to take the kids for the day. It has an extensive sand covering and small sand dunes they can play on. Strong currents and unexpected large waves can exist so keep an eye on them at all times.

FINALLY

A good beach to spend the day on with an easy, short walk to the beach without tiring you out like some others can.

FLAT ROCKS

HOW TO GET THERE 🔍

Bunurong Road,
Inverloch. From
Anderson Inlet,
follow Surf Parade
turning left into Cape
Paterson-Inverloch
Road which turns
into Bunurong Road.
Approximately 400 m
from the turn off is
a gravel car park on
the left. Park here and
walk over the dune to
the beach.

SNAPSHOT 🔍

PLATFORM
ROCK

TARGET FISH
AUSTRALIAN
 SALMON
GARFISH
SILVER TREVALLY
SQUID

BEST BAIT
PIPI
PEELED PRAWN
MAGGOTS
SILVER FISH
BLUEBAIT
SMALL SLITHERS
 OF PILCHARDS
SILVER WHITING
PILCHARDS

BEST LURES
ARTIFICIAL SQUID
 JIGS
METAL LURES.

BEST TIMES
HIGH AND LOW TIDE.

SEASONS

Australian salmon
Winter

Silver trevally
Winter

Garfish
Spring

Squid
Year round

Located just past Anderson Inlet, Flat Rocks is a great low tide fishing destination. Given the name due to the vast flat rocky configuration, anglers can walk onto the rocks to access deeper water. From the rock's edge, it is approximately 2 m deep, reaching 3 m with a good cast. Anglers fishing here need to be careful as the rocks are covered with Neptune's Necklace which is very slippery. Due to the shallowness of this location, fishing can be difficult in rough weather. If conditions are favourable however, anglers can fish for garfish, salmon, silver trevally and squid.

TACTICS

When the garfish are about, fishing for them should be done with a float setup. This can be tied from 10 lb leader with a blackfish float or quill ideal. Two or three BB size split shot sinkers can be crimped on the leader with a size 10 or 12 long shank hook ideal. Berley is essential to attract them to the area. Anglers on the look for something more sizeable can fish for salmon and silver trevally. These two species are often caught together on a paternoster rig. Due to the heavy reef, the rig should be tied

from 20 lb leader with size 1/0 long shank or suicide hooks. Squid are a common catch by those using a baited jig. This should be fitted with a silver whiting bait suspended under a float and cast as far as possible. A 9 to 10 ft surf rod is ideal when casting baited jigs. For artificial jigs a 7 ft spin rod or egi rod will suit. This should be coupled with a 2500 series reel that's loaded with 6 or 8 lb braid.

BAITS AND LURES

Garfish respond well to peeled prawn, maggots and silver fish while for salmon and silver trevally the most effective baits are pipi, bluebait and small slithers of pilchards. Metal lures are also popular for these species. For calamari use a whole silver whiting threaded onto the squid prong or artificial jigs with a red foil belly.

BEST TIDE/TIMES

Low tide is the best time for squid and garfish while high tide is productive for salmon and silver trevally.

AMENITIES

There are no immediate amenities in the area. Toilets, rubbish bins and shops are located in the township of Andersons Inlet.

KIDS AND FAMILIES

The sandy beach is a good location for children to play but it is recommended they do not go on the rocks as they are very slippery and unsafe.

FINALLY

This location is very productive, providing anglers fish during the peak times.

ANDERSONS INLET

🔍 HOW TO GET THERE

Anderson Inlet is located at Inverloch; access to the beach is good depending on where you park your car. There is plenty of car parking along Surf Parade. You can also park at the boat ramp located on the Esplanade and fish from the jetty.

🔍 SNAPSHOT

PLATFORM
BEACH/SURF

TARGET FISH
SALMON
WHITING
SILVER TREVALLY
PINKIE SNAPPER
GUMMY SHARK

BEST BAIT
PIPI
MUSSEL
BLUEBAIT
WHITEBAIT
PILCHARDS
SALMON FILLET
TREVALLY FILLET
SQUID

BEST LURES
METAL SLUGS
SOFT PLASTIC
MINNOWS

BEST TIMES
HIGH TIDE.

SEASONS

Australian salmon
May to July

Silver trevally
January to February

King George whiting
Summer

Gummy sharks
Year round

Pinkie snapper
Summer

Mulloway
Summer

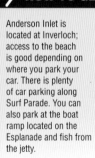

Anderson Inlet supports a wide variety of species but it is the whiting, salmon and trevally along with gummy sharks and pinkie snapper that are regularly targeted. Walking the length of the inlet along the sand is a fantastic way to experience the fishing. Anglers can work the shoreline until they find patches of fish. The edge of the inlet is predominantly sand with a few reef patches where fish congregate during certain times of the year.

TACTICS

There are three main locations to fish at Inverloch. These include the mouth of the entrance, Pensioner's Corner and the Boat Ramp jetty. Salmon provide plenty of light tackle entertainment during the cooler months and are mainly caught around the mouth of the entrance. The prime time to fish here is from the bottom of the low tide to half tide which is when you'll have to get off the rocks or you'll become surrounded by water. Fishing from the sand at Pensioner's Corner is highly productive for whiting during the high tide. Pensioner's Corner is one of the most productive locations as it provides anglers with easy casting distance into the main body of the channel. To be successful on whiting, a paternoster rig or running sinker rig works well. The boat ramp jetty is also a worthy fishing location during a high tide. Due to the force of the current, the ideal time to fish it is an hour each side of the high tide change.

BAITS AND LURES

Salmon will respond well to pipi, bluebait, whitebait and pilchards. Silver trevally and whiting prefer softer baits where pipi and mussels will work well. If you're fishing for pinkie snapper pilchards are the most popular baits while squid will stay on the hook longer. Metal lures work well on the salmon as do soft plastics on the pinkie snapper. Gummy sharks will sniff out oilier baits and will be best tempted with fresh fish fillets.

BEST TIDE/TIMES

When fishing for whiting, the last of the run out tide and last of the run in tides tend to be more productive. At the entrance, the salmon school up in numbers during the last of the run in tide. Fishing the run out will allow you further access to the main channel and still produce some good fish.

AMENITIES

Anderson Inlet has plenty of toilet blocks along the main foreshore. Rubbish bins are located in the car parks and at the boat ramp. Food shops and a tackle store are located in the main town which is only a few hundred metres from the foreshore.

KIDS AND FAMILIES

Anderson Inlet is a popular holiday destination for families during the summer months. The beaches are great for children to play and fish from although fast and strong currents do exist. Parental supervision is a must.

FINALLY

Anderson Inlet can offer all anglers some very productive fishing. If you're heading down for the day or the weekend, this location has it all. From night fishing to spinning from the sand, anglers can vary their fishing to cover a wide range of species.

Venus Bay can be accessed from many locations depending on which beach you have chosen to fish. From Inverloch, follow Inverloch-Venus Bay Road into Tarwin Lower. Follow Tarwin Lower Roa to Jupiter Boulevard then choose which beach you want to fish. For beach 1 take Surf Drive, Beach 2 take Inlet View Rd, for Beach 3 take No.3 Beach Road, Beach 4 take No.4 Beach Road and for beach5 take No.5 Beach Road.

Comprising of five beaches, Venus Bay see's four main species inhabit its waters. These include yellow-eye mullet, Australian salmon, gummy shark and silver trevally. Yellow-eye mullet and silver trevally are a common catch in the shore break with the odd gummy shark encountered by those putting in the time to fish throughout the night during full moon phases. When the salmon arrive, they can be in quite respectable numbers. Venus Bay is often known for delivering some monster salmon from time to time with fish up to three kilograms being a common catch throughout winter.

TACTICS
Yellow eye mullet and silver trevally are caught right in the shore break and respond really well to berley. This can be as simple as placing some berley pellets into an onion bag and leaving it on the sand to wash into the surf with each retreating wave. Due to their size, a light 7 ft spin rod with a 2500 series reel loaded with 6 lb braid is all that's required. Both species have a small soft mouth whereby a size 10 long shank hook will work well. Fish for salmon with a 12 ft surf rod and rig up a two hook paternoster made from a 20 lb leader. Spinning for salmon is also a popular affair nowadays with plenty of anglers getting in on the action. A 9 ft shore spin rod with 4000 series reel loaded with 10 lb braid is all that's required.

BAITS AND LURES
Salmon respond well to bluebait, whitebait, fresh pipi and pilchard. They can also be targeted on lures – namely metal slugs, surf poppers and minnow style soft plastics retrieved at high speeds. Gummy sharks should be targeted with oily baits such as trevally, fresh salmon and eel fillets. Yellow-eye mullet and silver trevally will take very small baits. Pilchard fillet and pipi baits are the favourites.

BEST TIDE/TIMES
A rising tide is always going to be the more productive time to fish for all species with overcast days or during first light for salmon. Gummy shark are traditionally caught during the night with the lead up and down from the full moon the prime times of the month.

AMENITIES
Beach 1 and 5 both have toilet blocks located in the car parks while the rest of the beaches do not. The township of Venus Bay has shops and tackle can be purchased. There are also rubbish bins located in each car park.

KIDS AND FAMILIES
The Venus Bay beaches are ideal for families. Whether it is just for a day at the beach or to go fishing, Venus Bay can accommodate every level of angler. Should children be swimming, care must be taken as strong swells and undercurrents are common.

FINALLY
Venus Bay and its comprising beaches are quite peaceful and can be very productive in season. Anglers that like to get the early worm will have most success and often get to the deeper gutters before the rest of the crowds arrive.

FISHING KNOTS

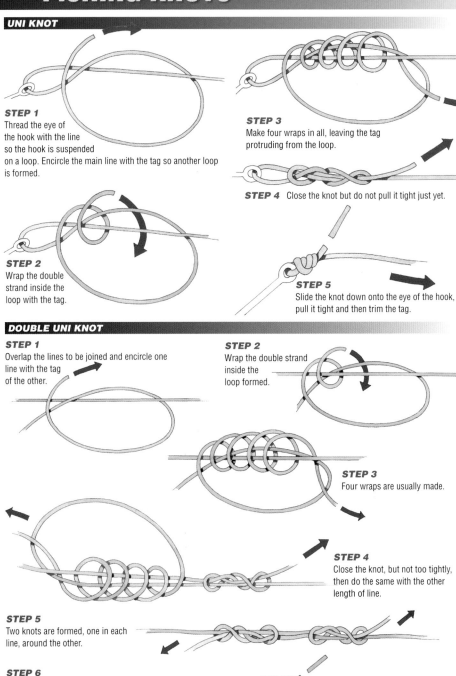

UNI KNOT

STEP 1
Thread the eye of
the hook with the line
so the hook is suspended
on a loop. Encircle the main line with the tag so another loop
is formed.

STEP 2
Wrap the double
strand inside the
loop with the tag.

STEP 3
Make four wraps in all, leaving the tag
protruding from the loop.

STEP 4 Close the knot but do not pull it tight just yet.

STEP 5
Slide the knot down onto the eye of the hook,
pull it tight and then trim the tag.

DOUBLE UNI KNOT

STEP 1
Overlap the lines to be joined and encircle one
line with the tag
of the other.

STEP 2
Wrap the double strand
inside the
loop formed.

STEP 3
Four wraps are usually made.

STEP 4
Close the knot, but not too tightly,
then do the same with the other
length of line.

STEP 5
Two knots are formed, one in each
line, around the other.

STEP 6
Slide the knots together, tighten
each in turn, and trim the tags.

LOCKED BLOOD KNOT

STEP 1
Thread the eye of your hook or swivel and twist the tag and main line together.

STEP 2
Complete three to six twists and thread the tag back through the first twist. The heavier your line, the less twists you will use.

STEP 3
Pull the line so that the knot begins to form, but not up tight yet as it will make an unlocked half blood which may slip. Lock the knot by threading the tag through the open loop that has formed at the top of the knot.

STEP 4
Pull the knot up firmly. Should a loop form within the knot, simply pull on the tag until it disappears.

COMMON SNELL

STEP 1
Make the configuration shown.

STEP 2
Pull the loop down to create another smaller loop as shown.

STEP 3
Keep wrapping the shank of the hook and the tag.

STEP 4
Keep wrapping until the desired number of wraps are in place.

STEP 5
Pull the main line and the tag until the knot is formed.

STEP 5
It is preferred that the snell is formed down a little from the eye so chances of separation by a roughly turned or sharp eye are reduced. Trim the tag.

FISHING KNOTS

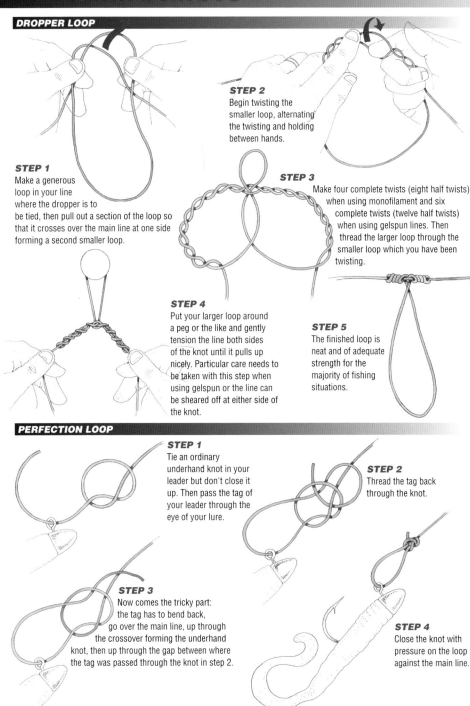

DROPPER LOOP

STEP 1
Make a generous
loop in your line
where the dropper is to
be tied, then pull out a section of the loop so
that it crosses over the main line at one side
forming a second smaller loop.

STEP 2
Begin twisting the
smaller loop, alternating
the twisting and holding
between hands.

STEP 3
Make four complete twists (eight half twists)
when using monofilament and six
complete twists (twelve half twists)
when using gelspun lines. Then
thread the larger loop through the
smaller loop which you have been
twisting.

STEP 4
Put your larger loop around
a peg or the like and gently
tension the line both sides
of the knot until it pulls up
nicely. Particular care needs to
be taken with this step when
using gelspun or the line can
be sheared off at either side of
the knot.

STEP 5
The finished loop is
neat and of adequate
strength for the
majority of fishing
situations.

PERFECTION LOOP

STEP 1
Tie an ordinary
underhand knot in your
leader but don't close it
up. Then pass the tag of
your leader through the
eye of your lure.

STEP 2
Thread the tag back
through the knot.

STEP 3
Now comes the tricky part:
the tag has to bend back,
go over the main line, up through
the crossover forming the underhand
knot, then up through the gap between where
the tag was passed through the knot in step 2.

STEP 4
Close the knot with
pressure on the loop
against the main line.

RUNNING SINKER RIG

A running sinker rig is one of the most versatile rigs that can be used for Western Port or where an area is affected by fast current. Locations such as Stony Point pier require the use of this style of rig. This rig is mainly used when targeting gummy sharks, elephant fish and snapper.

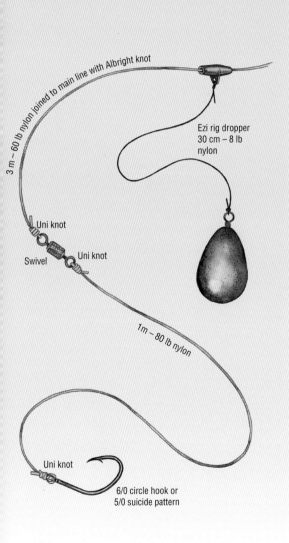

3 m – 60 lb nylon joined to main line with Albright knot

Ezi rig dropper 30 cm – 8 lb nylon

Uni knot

Swivel

Uni knot

1m – 80 lb nylon

Uni knot

6/0 circle hook or 5/0 suicide pattern

GARFISH FLOAT RIG

Garfish are a top water feeder, meaning they swim and feed just under the water's surface. When targeting them, a float setup will allow a bait to be suspended in their feeding zone. The float will also act as a bite indicator for anglers to see when the bait has been taken and the fish is hooked.

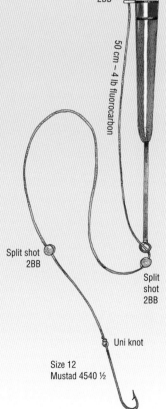

Quill float

Split shot 2BB

50 cm – 4 lb fluorocarbon

Split shot 2BB

Split shot 2BB

Uni knot

Size 12 Mustad 4540 ½

GUMMY SHARK RIG

SQUID FLOAT RIG

Landbased anglers fishing for calamari don't always get the casting distance required when using an artificial jig. The baited float rig is highly effective and allows the bait to be suspended by the float to hover just above the weed beds. The float will need to be set according to the depth fished, and when right works exceptionally well.

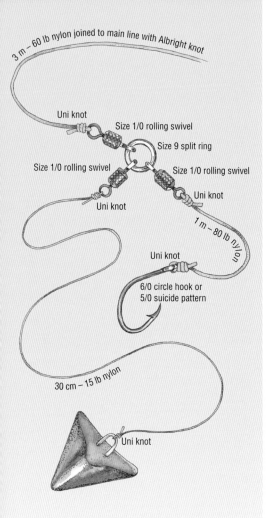

3 m – 60 lb nylon joined to main line with Albright knot

Uni knot

Size 1/0 rolling swivel

Size 9 split ring

Size 1/0 rolling swivel

Size 1/0 rolling swivel

Uni knot

Uni knot

1 m – 80 lb nylon

Uni knot

6/0 circle hook or 5/0 suicide pattern

30 cm – 15 lb nylon

Uni knot

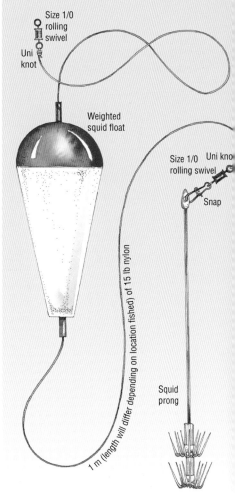

Size 1/0 rolling swivel

Uni knot

Weighted squid float

Size 1/0 rolling swivel

Uni knot

Snap

1 m (length will differ depending on location fished) of 15 lb nylon

Squid prong

The gummy shark rig is mainly used in surf fishing situations. This rig has been manipulated to allow the sinker to sit in the sand without needing too much drag pressure bestowed on the reel as with a running sinker rig. The use of the swivel and split rig setup is to prevent line twist in a strong swell or side wash situation. Strictly used for gummy shark, it is a highly recommended rig to use

LANDBASED FISHING RIGS

WHITING PATERNOSTER RIG

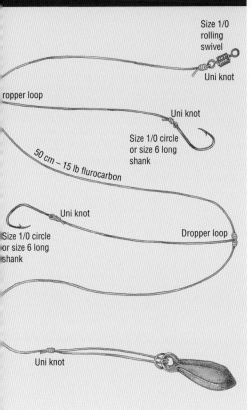

Size 1/0 rolling swivel

Uni knot

ropper loop

Uni knot

Size 1/0 circle or size 6 long shank

50 cm – 15 lb flurocarbon

Uni knot

Size 1/0 circle or size 6 long shank

Dropper loop

Uni knot

A paternoster rig is one of the most commonly used rigs in fishing but there are plenty of variations about. The whiting version is made to allow the baits to sit just above the weed beds. Designed to be used with circle hooks, this rig is perfect when fishing in fast current situations. Not only good for whiting but this rig will also catch trevally, flathead and salmon.

SALMON PATERNOSTER RIG

Another variation of the paternoster rig, the salmon paternoster is made from a little heavier tackle than the whiting. This rig is ideal for surf fishing as it allows two baits to be suspended in the water column. This rig is strictly used for surf fishing and is ideal for salmon.

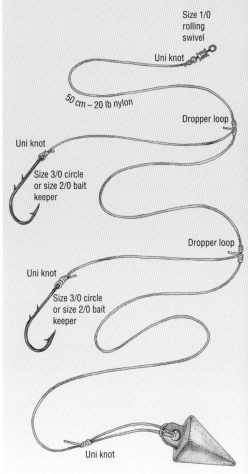

Size 1/0 rolling swivel

Uni knot

50 cm – 20 lb nylon

Dropper loop

Uni knot

Size 3/0 circle or size 2/0 bait keeper

Dropper loop

Uni knot

Size 3/0 circle or size 2/0 bait keeper

Uni knot

BAIT PRESENTATION

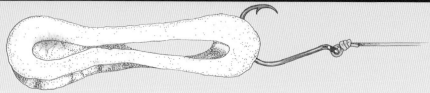

CALAMARI RING

A calamari ring bait is one of the most effective and simplest ways to fish with calamari for bait. Rings are mainly used when fishing in fast current situations so as to prevent the bait from spinning in the current. Once pinned on the hooks, the ring will sit in the current and slowly sway with the pressure of the water. This bait presentation is perfect for snapper, elephant fish, gummy shark and mulloway.

FILLET BAIT

Fillets are fantastic to use if fresh. They are easy to cut from a whole fish and can be pinned using two hooks. In fast tidal areas, fillet baits may spin, causing line twist and put off fish from taking it. They are best used at locations such as Stockyard Point or Lang Lang.
This bait presentation is most effective on snapper and gummy sharks.

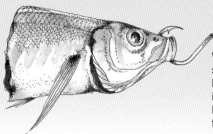

FISH HEAD

Whole fish heads are used when targeting big fish. Heads should be cut from the pectoral fin and pinned using one hook through the mouth region. Head baits can be used in any location and sit well when used with a single hook. Fish heads are suitable for gummy sharks, snapper and toothy sharks.

HALF PILCHARD

A half pilchard is a neat little bait that can be used for a variety of species. The bait itself should be cut in half and pinned using a single hook with a half hitch around the tail section to keep it straight. Baiting this way is ideal when fishing the surf for salmon.

BAIT PRESENTATION

When fishing for whiting, pipi baits are the most popular bait used. When placing on the hook, it is imperative that they be neatly pinned, then wrapped and re-pinned on the hook. This prevents them from being taken off the hook. Perfect for whiting, salmon and silver trevally.

SQUID STRIP

Often, big baits can deter fish which is where a small strip of squid is ideal. Using either a tentacle or straight piece of calamari hood, the squid strip can be pinned on either a single hook or two hook setup. Squid strips are ideal for targeting snapper, gummy sharks and elephant fish.

WHOLE BLUEBAIT OR PILCHARD

Bluebait or pilchards can also be fished whole and are recommended for big salmon. This bait is recommended for salmon in the surf or snapper and flathead in calmer water. If not pinned on the hooks correctly, they can spin in the current. They can be used with either a single hook rig or twin hook rig. Either way, they will require a half hitch on the tail to keep inline.

WHOLE FISH

When fishing for snapper a whole bait is recommended. This bait, regardless of type of fish used, must be rigged using two hooks to hold straight and to prevent from falling off the hook. One hook should be placed in the head while the other in the tail section with a half hitch around the tail. This presentation is ideal for all snapper situations.

TARGET FISH ID GUIDE

AUSTRALIAN SALMON

BAG LIMIT
20

MINIMUM LENGTH
21 cm

GROWS TO
90 cm / 9 kg

BARRACOUTA

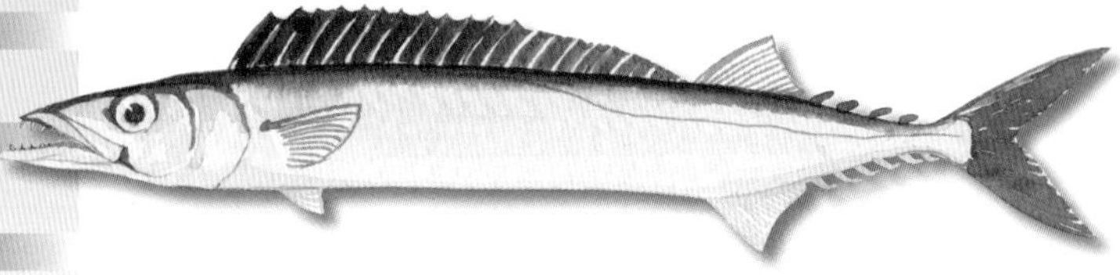

BAG LIMIT
20

MINIMUM LENGTH
No size limit

GROWS TO
130 cm / 5 kg

BLUE MORWONG

BAG LIMIT
5

MINIMUM LENGTH
23 cm

GROWS TO
140 cm / 40 kg

BLUE THROATED WRASSE

BAG LIMIT
5 *Total of one species or more*

MINIMUM LENGTH
27 cm

GROWS TO
40 cm / 1 kg

BREAM FAMILY

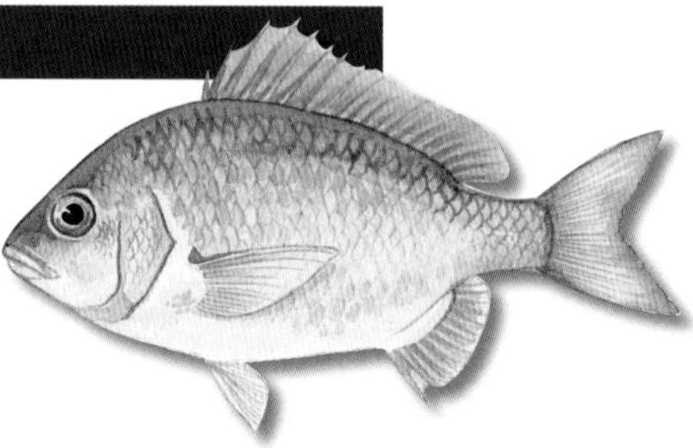

BAG LIMIT
10

MINIMUM LENGTH
28 cm

GROWS TO
60 cm / 3.5 kg

TARGET FISH ID GUIDE

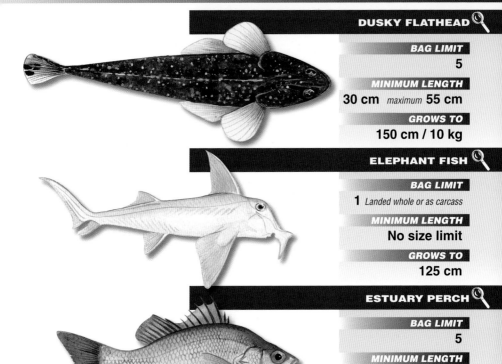

DUSKY FLATHEAD 🔍

BAG LIMIT
5

MINIMUM LENGTH
30 cm *maximum* 55 cm

GROWS TO
150 cm / 10 kg

ELEPHANT FISH 🔍

BAG LIMIT
1 *Landed whole or as carcass*

MINIMUM LENGTH
No size limit

GROWS TO
125 cm

ESTUARY PERCH 🔍

BAG LIMIT
5

MINIMUM LENGTH
27 cm

GROWS TO
65 cm / 7.5 kg

FLOUNDER FAMILY 🔍

BAG LIMIT
20

MINIMUM LENGTH
23 cm

GROWS TO
50 cm / 1 kg

GUMMY SHARK 🔍

BAG LIMIT
2 *Landed whole or as carcass*

MINIMUM LENGTH
45 cm

GROWS TO
175 cm

TARGET FISH ID GUIDE

KING GEORGE WHITING

BAG LIMIT
20 *Landed whole or as carcass*

MINIMUM LENGTH
27 cm

GROWS TO
67 cm / 2 kg

LEATHERJACKET FAMILY

BAG LIMIT
20

MINIMUM LENGTH
No size limit

GROWS TO
60 cm

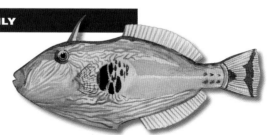

LING FAMILY

BAG LIMIT
5

MINIMUM LENGTH
30 cm

GROWS TO
110 cm / 8 kg

MULLET FAMILY

BAG LIMIT
40

MINIMUM LENGTH
No size limit

GROWS TO
80 cm / 5 kg

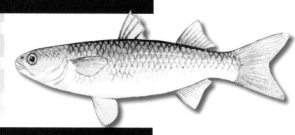

MULLOWAY

BAG LIMIT
5

MINIMUM LENGTH
60 cm

GROWS TO
180 cm / 60 kg

TARGET FISH ID GUIDE

SILVER TREVALLY

BAG LIMIT	20
MINIMUM LENGTH	20 cm
GROWS TO	100 cm / 11 kg

SNAPPER

BAG LIMIT	10
MINIMUM LENGTH	**28 cm** *no more than 3 greater than or equal to 40 cm*
GROWS TO	125 cm / 19 kg

SOUTHERN BLUE SPOT FLATHEAD

BAG LIMIT	20
MINIMUM LENGTH	27 cm
GROWS TO	100 cm / 8 kg

SQUID, OCTOPUS, CUTTLEFISH

BAG LIMIT	**10** *Total for one or more species*
MINIMUM LENGTH	No size limit
GROWS TO	*Varies between species*

TAILOR

BAG LIMIT	20
MINIMUM LENGTH	23 cm
GROWS TO	120 cm / 17 kg

TARGET FISH ID GUIDE

TIGER FLATHEAD

BAG LIMIT
20

MINIMUM LENGTH
27 cm

GROWS TO
65 cm / 2.5 kg

WRASSE FAMILY

BAG LIMIT
5 Total for one or more species

MINIMUM LENGTH
23 cm

GROWS TO
40 cm / 1 kg

YELLOW-EYE MULLET

BAG LIMIT
40

MINIMUM LENGTH
No minimum

GROWS TO
35 cm / 1 kg

YELLOWTAIL KINGFISH

BAG LIMIT
5

MINIMUM LENGTH
60 cm

GROWS TO
200 cm / 50 kg

BAIT

AUSTRALIAN ANCHOVY

PILCHARD

BLUE SPRAT

Bag limit: 40
No size limit
Grows to: 23 cm

PRAWN

Bag limit: 30 litres
5 litres just meat
Grows to: 30 cm

MUSSEL

Bag limit: 10 litres
1 litre if shucked

Limits do not apply to purchased bait

SEAFORD BAIT P/L

EST 1983

5979 7800

seafordbait@gmail.com

**WHOLESALE BAIT,
BERLEY & TACKLE**

OUR PRODUCTS
- Freshly processed at location WA
- IQF pilchards
- WA pilchard blocks
- Whole silver trevally
- Whole Bonito
- Whole Slimy Mackeral
- Quality South Australian pippies
- Blue and Whitebait
- Quality Silver whiting
- Sauries
- Californian Squid 1lb, 1KG
- Whole Arrow Squid
- Squid Heads
- Bottly Squid
- Garfish
- Yakkas
- Mussels, shell and meat
- Prawns
- Silverfish
- Berley pilchards
- Burley logs - 3 sizes
- Cuttlefish
- Cured Eel
- Octopus, Glassies, Bass Yabbies
- Beach Worms and much more